# Recollections
## Of
# Old Liverpool

*by*

James Stonehouse

# Recollections Of Old Liverpool
## by James Stonehouse



ISBN: 978-93-59392-75-2

**Published by**

# DOUBLE 9 BOOKS

2/13-B, Ansari Road
Daryaganj, New Delhi – 110002
info@double9books.com
www.double9books.com
Tel. 011-40042856

# ABOUT THE AUTHOR

James Stonehouse is an esteemed author known for his insightful writings that delve into the depths of history. His works captivate readers with vivid descriptions and meticulous attention to detail, transporting them to bygone eras. Through his writing, Stonehouse brings the past to life, painting a vibrant picture of the times he explores. With a passion for uncovering forgotten stories, James Stonehouse has dedicated himself to chronicling the rich tapestry of history, particularly focusing on the city of Liverpool. His book "Recollections of Old Liverpool" stands as a testament to his deep connection with the city, as he delves into its fascinating past, shedding light on its traditions, architecture, and the everyday lives of its inhabitants. Stonehouse's prose is both engaging and informative, offering readers a glimpse into a world that once was. His meticulous research and keen eye for historical accuracy ensure that his writings are not only entertaining but also educational, providing valuable insights into the social, cultural, and economic fabric of the times he explores. As an author, James Stonehouse possesses the ability to transport his readers through time, inviting them to walk alongside the characters and witness the events that shaped history. His passion for storytelling and his commitment to preserving the legacy of Liverpool make him a cherished figure in the realm of historical literature.

# CONTENTS

# PREFACE.

The "Recollections of Old Liverpool," contained in the following pages, appeared originally the *Liverpool Compass*, their publication extending over a period of several months.

When they were commenced it was intended to limit them to three, or at the most four, chapters, but such was the interest they created, that they were extended to their present length.

Those who have recorded the green memories of an old man, as told while seated by his humble "ingle nook" have endeavoured to adhere to his own words and mode of narration—hence the somewhat rambling and discursive style of these "Recollections"—a style which does not, in the opinion of many, by any means detract from their general interest.

The frontispiece is copied (by special permission) from part of a very finely-painted view of Liverpool, by Jenkinson, dated 1813, in the possession of Thomas Dawson, Esq., Rodney-street. The vignette of the Mill which stood at the North end of the St. James' Quarry in the title page, is from an original water colour drawing by an amateur (name unknown), dated 1821.

*November*, 1863.

# CHAPTER I.

I was born in Liverpool, on the 4th of June in 1769 or '70. I am consequently about ninety-three years old. My friends say I am a wonderful old man. I believe I am. I have always enjoyed such excellent health, that I do not know what the sensation is of a medical man putting his finger on my wrist. I have eaten and drunk in moderation, slept little, risen early, and kept a clear conscience before God and man. My memory is surprising. I am often astonished at myself in recalling to mind events, persons, and circumstances, that occurred so long ago as to be almost forgotten by everybody else.

I can recollect every occurrence that has fallen under my cognizance, since I was six years old. I do not remember so well events that have taken place during the last twenty or thirty years, as they seem confused to me; but whatever happened of which I had some knowledge during my boyish days and early manhood, is most vividly impressed upon my memory. My family have been long-livers. My father was ninety odd, when he died, my mother near that age at her death. My brother and sister are still living, are healthy, and, like myself, in comfortable circumstances.

I may be seen any fine day on the Pier-head or Landing-stage, accompanied by one of my dear great grandchildren; but you would not take me to be more than sixty by my air and appearance.

We lived in a street out of Church-street, nearly opposite St. Peter's. I was born there. At that time the churchyard was enclosed by trees, and the gravestones were erect. One by one the trees died or were destroyed by mischievous boys, and unfortunately they were not replaced. The church presented then a very pretty appearance. Within the last thirty years there was one tree standing nearly opposite to the Blue Coat School. When that tree died, I regretted its loss as of an old friend. The stocks were placed just within the rails, nearly opposite the present extensive premises occupied by the Elkingtons. Many and many a man have I seen seated in them for various light offences, though in many cases the punishment was heavy, especially if the culprit was obnoxious in any way, or had made himself so by his own conduct. The town boys were very cruel in my young days. It was a cruel time, and the effects of the slave-trade and privateering were visible in the conduct of the lower classes and of society generally.

Goodness knows the town boys are cruel now, but they are angels to what their predecessors were. I think education has done some good. All sorts of mischievous tricks used to be played upon the culprits in the stocks; and I have seen stout and sturdy fellows faint under the sufferings they endured. By the way, at the top of Marybone, there was once a large pond, called the Flashes, where there was a ducking-post and this was a favourite place of punishment when the Lynch Law of that time was carried out. I once saw a woman ducked there. She might have said with Queen Catherine:—

"Do with me what you will,
For any change must better my condition."

There was a terrible row caused once by the rescue of a woman from the Cuckstool. At one time it threatened to be serious. The mayor was dining at my father's, and I recollect he was sent for in a great hurry, and my father and his guests all went with him to the pond. The woman was nearly killed, and her life for long despaired of. She was taken to the Infirmary, on the top of Shaw's Brow, where St. George's Hall now stands. The way they ducked was this. A long pole, which acted as a lever, was placed on a post; at the end of the pole was a chair, in which the culprit was seated; and by ropes at the other end of the lever or pole, the culprit was elevated or dipped in the water at the mercy of the wretches who had taken upon themselves the task of executing punishment. The screams of the poor women who were ducked were frightful. There was a ducking tub in the House of Correction, which was in use in Mr. Howard's time. I once went with him through the prison (as I shall describe presently) and saw it there. It was not till 1804 or 1805 that it was done away with.

My father was owner and commander of the *Mary Ellen*. She was launched on the 4th of June, my birthday, and also the anniversary of our revered sovereign, George III. We used to keep his majesty's birthday in great style. The bells were set ringing, cannon fired, colours waved in the wind, and all the schools had holiday. We don't love the gracious Lady who presides over our destinies less than we did her august grandfather, but I am sure we do not keep her birthday as we did his. The *Mary Ellen* was launched on the 4th of June, 1775. She was named after and by my mother. The launch of this ship is about the first thing I can remember. The day's proceedings are indelibly fixed upon my memory. We went down to the place where the ship was built, accompanied by our friends. We made quite a little procession, headed by a drum and fife. My father and mother walked first, leading me by the hand. I had new clothes on, and I firmly believed that the joy bells were ringing solely because *our* ship was to be launched. The *Mary Ellen* was launched from a piece of open ground just beyond the present Salt-house Dock, then called, "the South Dock." I suppose the exact place would be somewhere about the middle of the present King's Dock. The bank on which the ship was built sloped down to the river. There was a slight boarding round her. There were several other ships and smaller vessels building near her; amongst others, a frigate which afterwards did great damage to the enemy during the French war. The government frequently gave orders for ships to be built at Liverpool. The view up the river was very fine. There were few houses to be seen southward. The mills on the Aigburth-road were the principal objects.

It was a pretty sight to see the *Mary Ellen* launched. There were crowds of people present, for my father was well-known and very popular. When the ship moved off there was a great cheer raised. I was so excited at the great "splash" which was made, that I cried, and was for a time inconsolable, because they would not launch the ship again, so that I might witness another great "splash." I can, in my mind's eye, see "the splash" of the *Mary Ellen* even now. I really believe the displacement of the water on that occasion opened the doors of observation in my mind. After the launch there was great festivity and hilarity. I believe I made myself very ill with the quantity of fruit and good things I became possessed of. While the *Mary Ellen* was fitting-up for sea, I was often taken on board. In her hold were long shelves with ring-bolts in rows in several places. I used to run along these shelves, little thinking what dreadful scenes would be enacted upon them. The fact is that the *Mary Ellen* was destined for the African trade, in which she made many very successful voyages. In 1779, however, she was converted into a privateer. My father, at the present time, would not, perhaps, be thought very respectable; but I assure you he was so considered in those days. So many people in Liverpool were, to use an old and trite sea-phrase, "tarred with the same brush" that these occupations were scarcely, indeed, were not at all, regarded as anything derogatory from a man's character. In fact, during the privateering time, there was scarcely a man, woman, or child in Liverpool, of any standing, that did not hold a share in one of these ships. Although a slave captain, and afterwards a privateer, my father was a kind and just man—a good father, husband, and friend. His purse and advice were always ready to help and save, and he was, consequently, much respected by the merchants with whom he had intercourse. I have been told that he was quite a different man at sea, that there he was harsh, unbending and stern, but still just. How he used to rule the turbulent spirits of his crews I don't know, but certain it is that he never wanted men when other Liverpool ship-owners were short of hands. Many of his seamen sailed voyage after voyage with him. It was these old hands that were attached to him who I suspect kept the others in subjection. The men used to make much of me. They made me little sea toys, and always brought my mother and myself presents from Africa, such as parrots, monkeys, shells, and articles of the natives' workmanship. I recollect very well, after the *Mary Ellen* had been converted into a privateer, that, on her return from a successful West Indian cruise, the mate of the ship, a great big fellow, named Blake, and who was one of the roughest and most ungainly men ever seen, would insist upon my mother accepting a beautiful chain, of Indian workmanship, to which was attached the miniature of a very lovely woman. I doubt the rascal did not come by it very honestly, neither was a costly bracelet that one of my father's best hands (once a Northwich salt-flatman) brought home for my baby sister. This man would insist upon putting it on the baby somewhere, in spite of all my mother and the nurse could say; so, as its thigh was the nearest approach to the bracelet in size of any of its little limbs, there the bracelet was clasped. It fitted tightly and baby evidently did not approve of the ornament. My mother took it off when the man left. I have it now. This man used to tell queer stories about the salt trade, and the fortunes made therein, and how they used to land salt on stormy and dark nights on the Cheshire or Lancashire borders, or into boats alongside, substituting the same weight of water as the salt taken out, so that the cargo should pass muster at the Liverpool Custom House. The duty was payable at the works, and the cargo was re-weighed in Liverpool. If found over weight, the merchant had to pay extra duty; and if short weight, he had to make up the deficiency in salt. The trade required a large capital, and was, therefore, in few hands. One house is known to have paid as much as £30,000 for duty in six weeks. My grandfather told me that in 1732 (time of William and Mary), when he was a boy, the duty on salt was levied for a term of years at first, but made perpetual in the third year of George II. Sir R. Walpole proposed to set apart the proceeds of the impost for his majesty's use.

The Salt houses occupied the site of Orford-street (called after Mr. Blackburne's seat in Cheshire). I have often heard my grandfather speak of them as an intolerable nuisance, causing, at times, the town to be enveloped in steam and smoke. These Salt houses raised such an outcry at last that in 1703 they were removed to Garston, Mr. Blackburne having obtained an act of Parliament relative to them for that purpose.

The fine and coarse salts manufactured in Liverpool were in the proportion of fifteen tons of Northwich or Cheshire rock-salt to forty-five tons of seawater, to produce thirteen tons of salt. To show how imperishable salt must be, if such testimony be needed, it is a fact that, in the yard of a warehouse occupied by a friend of mine in Orford-street, the soil was always damp previous to a change of weather, and a well therein was of no use whatever, except for cleansing purposes, so brackish was the water.

To return to the launch. After the feasting was over my father treated our friends to the White House and Ranelagh Tea Gardens, which stood at the top of Ranelagh-street. The site is now occupied by the Adelphi Hotel. The gardens extended a long way back. Warren-street is formed out of them. These gardens were very tastefully arranged in beds and borders, radiating from a centre in which was a Chinese temple, which served as an orchestra for a band to play in. Round the sides of the garden, in a thicket of lilacs and laburnums, the beauty of which, in early summer, was quite remarkable, were little alcoves or bowers wherein parties took tea or stronger drinks. About half-way up the garden, the place where the Warren-street steps are now, there used to be a large pond or tank wherein were fish of various sorts. These fish were so tame that they would come to the surface to be fed. This fish feeding was a very favourite amusement with those who frequented the garden. In the tank were some carp of immense size, and so fat they could hardly swim. Our servant-man used to take me to the Ranelagh Gardens every fine afternoon, as it was a favourite lounge. Over the garden door was written—

> "You are welcome to walk here I say,
> But if flower or fruit you pluck
> One shilling you must pay."

The garden paling was carried up Copperas-hill (called after the Copperas Works, removed in 1770, after long litigation) across to Brownlow-hill, a white ropery extending behind the palings. To show how remarkably neighbourhoods alter by time and circumstance, I recollect it was said that Lord Molyneux, while hunting, once ran a hare down Copperas-hill. A young lady, Miss Harvey, who resided near the corner, went out to see what was the cause of the disturbance she heard, when observing the hare, she turned it back. Miss Harvey used to say "the gentlemen swore terribly" at her for spoiling their sport. This was not seventy years ago!

To return to the Ranelagh Gardens. There was, at the close of the gala nights, as they were called, a display of fireworks. They were let off on the terrace. I went to see the last exhibition which took place in 1780. There was, on that occasion, a concert in which Miss Brent, (who was, by the way, a great favourite) appeared. Jugglers used to exhibit in the concert-room, which was very capacious, as it would hold at least 800 to 1000 persons. This concert-room was also used as a dinner-room on great occasions, and also as a town ball-room. Stephens gave his lecture on "Heads" in it very frequently.

G. A. Stephens was an actor, who, after playing about in the provincial highways and bye-ways of the dramatic world, went to London, where he was engaged at Covent Garden in second and third rate parts. He was a man of dissipated habits, but a jovial and merry companion. He wrote a great many very clever songs, which he sang with great humour. He got the idea of the lectures on "Heads" from a working man about one of the theatres, whom he saw imitating some of the members of the corporation of the town in which he met with him. Stephens, who was quick and ready with his pen, in a short time got up his lecture, which he delivered all through England, Scotland, Ireland, and America. He realised upwards of £10,000, which he took care of, as he left that sum behind him at his death, in 1784. He was at the time, a completely worn-out, imbecile old man. Many of the leading actors of his day followed up the lecture on "Heads," in which they signally failed to convey the meaning of the author. I saw him, and was very much amused; but I do not think he would be tolerated in the present day. The elder Mathews evidently caught the idea of his "At Homes" from Stephens's lecture.

Brownlow-hill was so called after Mr. Lawrence Brownlow, a gentleman who held much property thereabout. Brownlow-hill was a very pleasant walk. There were gardens on it, as, also, on Mount Pleasant, then called Martindale's-hill, of which our friend Mr. Roscoe has sung so sweetly. Martindale's-hill was quite a country walk when I was a little boy. There was also a pleasant walk over the Moss Lake Fields to Edge Hill. Where the Eye and Ear Infirmary stands there was a stile and a foot-path to the Moss Lake Brook, across it was a wooden foot bridge. The path afterwards diverged to Smithdown-lane. The path-road also went on to Pembroke-place, along the present course of Crown-street. I have heard my father speak of an attempt being made to rob him on passing over the stile which stood where now you find the King William Tavern. He drew his sword (a weapon commonly worn by gentlemen of the time) which so frightened the thieves that they ran away, and, in their flight, went into a pit of water, into which my father also ran in the darkness which prevailed. The thieves roared loudly for help, which my father did not stop to accord them. He, being a good swimmer, soon got out, leaving the thieves to extricate themselves as they could. There were several very pleasant country walks which went up to Low-hill through Brownlow-street, and by Love-lane (now Fairclough-lane). I recollect going along Love-lane many a time with my dear wife, when we were sweethearting. We used to go to Low-hill and thence along Everton-road (then called Everton-lane), on each side of which was a row of large trees, and we returned by Loggerhead's-lane (now Everton Crescent), and so home by Richmond-row, (called after Dr. Sylvester Richmond, a physician greatly esteemed and respected.) I recollect very well the brook that ran along the present Byrom-street, whence the tannery on the right-hand side was supplied with water. At the bottom of Richmond-row used to be the kennels of the Liverpool Hunt Club. They were at one time kept on the North-shore.

# CHAPTER II.

I was very sorry when the Ranelagh Gardens were broken up. The owner, Mr. Gibson, was the brother of the Mr. Gibson who kept the Folly Gardens at the bottom of Folly-lane (now Islington) and top of Shaw's Brow (called after Mr. Alderman Shaw, the great potter, who lived in Dale-street, at the corner of Fontenoy-street—whose house is still standing). Many a time have I played in the Folly Tea Gardens. It was a pretty place, and great was the regret of the inhabitants of Liverpool when it was resolved to build upon it. The Folly was closed in 1785. Mr. Philip Christian built his house, now standing at the corner of Christian-street, of the bricks of which the Tavern was constructed. The Folly was a long two-storied house, with a tower or gazebo at one end. Gibson, it was said, was refused permission to extend the size of his house, so "he built it upright," as he said "he could not build it along." The entrance to the Gardens was from Folly-lane, up a rather narrow passage. I rather think the little passage at the back of the first house in Christian-street was a part of it. You entered through a wooden door and went along a shrubberied path which led to the Tavern. Folly-lane (now Islington) was a narrow country lane, with fields and gardens on both sides. I recollect there was a small gardener's cottage where the Friends' Institute now stands; and there was a lane alongside. That lane is now called "King-street-lane, Soho." I remember my mother, one Sunday, buying me a lot of apples for a penny, which were set out on a table at the gate. There were a great many apple, pear, and damson trees in the garden. When the Friends' Institute was building I heard of the discovery of an old cottage, which had been hidden from view as it were for many years. I went to see it—the sight of it brought tears in my old eyes, for I recognised the place at once, and thought of my good and kind mother, and her friendly and loving ways. Where the timber-yard was once in Norton-street, there used to be a farm-house. The Moss-lake Stream ran by it on its way to Byrom-street. I can very well remember Norton-street and the streets thereabout being formed. At the top of Stafford-street, laid out at the same time, there was a smithy and forge; the machinery of the bellows was turned by the water from the Moss-lake Brook, which ran just behind the present Mill Tavern. There the water was collected in an extensive dam, in shape like a "Ruperts' Drop," the overflow turned some of the mill machinery. Many and many a fish have I caught out of that mill-dam. The fields at the back, near Folly-lane, were flooded one winter, and frozen over, when I and many other boys went to slide on them.

The Folly Gardens were very tastefully laid out. Mr. Gibson was a spirited person, and spared no expense to keep the place in order. There were two bowling-greens in it, and a skittle-alley. There was a cockpit once, outside the gardens; but that was many years before my time. It was laid bare when they were excavating for Islington Market. When I was a boy its whereabouts was not known; it was supposed to have been of great antiquity. How time brings things to light! The gardens were full of beautiful flowers and noble shrubs. There was a large fish-pond in the middle of a fine lawn, and around it were benches for the guests, who, on fine summer evenings, used to sit and smoke, and drink a sort of compound called "braggart," which was made of ale, sugar, spices, and eggs, I believe. I used to sail a little ship in that pond, made for me by the mate of the *Mary Ellen*. I one day fell in, and was pulled out by Mr. Gibson himself, who fortunately happened to be passing near at hand. He took me in his arms dripping as I was, into the tavern and I was put to bed, while a man was sent down to Church-street, to acquaint my parents with my disaster, and for dry clothes. My mother came up in a terrible fright, but my father only laughed heartily at the accident, saying he had been overboard three times before he was my age. He must have had a charmed life, if he spoke true, for I don't think I could have been above eight years old then. My father was well acquainted with Mr. Gibson, and after I had got on my dry clothes, he took us up to the top of the Gazebo, or look-out tower. It was a beautiful evening, and the air was quite calm and clear. The view was magnificent. We could see Beeston Castle quite plainly, and Halton Castle also, as well as the Cheshire shore and the Welsh mountains. The view out seaward was truly fine. Young as I was, I was greatly struck with the whole scene. It was just at the time when the Folly Fair was held, and the many objects at our feet made the whole view one of intense interest. The rooms in the tower were then filled with company. Folly Fair was held on the open space of ground afterwards used as Islington Market. Booths were erected opposite the Infirmary and in Folly Lane. It was like all such assemblages—a great deal of noise, drunkenness, debauchery, and foolishness. But fairs were certainly different then from what they have been of late years. They are now conducted in a far more orderly manner than they were formerly. I went to a large one some years ago, in Manchester, and, on comparing it with those of my young days, I could hardly believe it was a fair. It seemed to be only the ghost of one, so grim and ghastly were the proceedings.

I recollect the celebrated Mr. John Howard, "the philanthropist," coming to Liverpool in 1787. He had a letter of introduction to my father, and was frequently at our house. He was a thin, spare man, with an expressive eye and a determined look. He used to go every day to the Tower Prison at the bottom of Water-street; and he exerted himself greatly to obtain a reform in the atrocious abuses which then existed in prison discipline. In the present half-century there has been great progress made in the improvement of prison discipline, health, and economy. Where formerly existed notorious and disgraceful abuses, the most abject misery, and the very depth of dirt, we find good management, cleanliness, reformatory measures, and firm steps taken to reclaim both the bodies and souls of the erring. It is a most strange circumstance that the once gross and frightful abuses of the prison system did not *force* themselves upon the notice of government—did not attract the attention of local rulers, and cry out themselves for change. Still more strange is it that, although Mr Howard in 1787, and again in 1795, and Mr. James Nield (whose acquaintance I also made in 1803), pointed out so distinctly the abuses that existed in our prisons, the progress of reform therein was strangely slow, and moved with most apathetic steps. Howard lifted up the veil and exposed to light the iniquities prevalent within our prison walls; but no rapid change was noticeable in consequence of his appalling revelations. To show how careless the authorities were about these matters, we can see what Mr. Nield said eight years after Mr. Howard's second visit, in 1795, in his celebrated letters to Dr. Lettsom, who, by the way, resided in Camberwell Grove, Surrey, in the house said to have belonged to the uncle of George Barnwell. Now, it should be borne in mind that Mr. Howard actually received the freedom of the borough, with many compliments upon his exertions in the cause of the poor inmates of the gaol, and yet few or no important steps were taken to remedy the glaring evils which he pointed out. Some feeble reforms certainly did take place immediately after his first and second visits to Liverpool, but a retrograde movement succeeded, and things relapsed into their usual jog-trot way of dirt and disorder. When Mr. Howard received the freedom of the borough an immense fuss was made about him; people used to follow him in the street, and he was *feted* and invited to dinners and parties; and there was no end of speechifying. But what did it all come to? Why, nothing, except a little cleaning out of passages and whitewashing of walls. I went with Mr. Howard several times, over the Tower Prison, and also with Mr. Nield, in 1803. As it then appeared I will try to describe it.

The keeper of the Tower or Borough Gaol, which stood at the bottom of Water-street in 1803, was Mr. Edward Frodsham, who was also sergeant-at-mace. His salary was £130 per annum. His fees were 4s. for criminal prisoners, and 4s. 6d. for debtors. The Rev. Edward Monk was the chaplain. His salary was £31 10s. per annum; but his ministrations did not appear to be very efficacious, as, on one occasion, when Mr. Nield went to the prison chapel in company with two of the borough magistrates, he found, out of one hundred and nine prisoners, only six present at service. The sick were attended by a surgeon from the Dispensary, in consideration of 12 guineas per annum, contributed by the corporation to that most praiseworthy institution. There was a sort of sick ward in the Tower, but it was a wretched place, being badly ventilated and extremely dirty. When Mr. Nield and I visited the prison in 1803, we did not find the slightest order or regulation. The prisoners were not classed, nor indeed, separated; men and women, boys and girls, debtor and felon, young and old, were all herded together, meeting daily in the courtyards of the prison. The debtors certainly had a yard to themselves, but they had free access to the felon's yard, and mixed unrestrainedly with them. The prison allowance was a three-penny loaf of 1lb. 3oz. to each prisoner daily. Convicts were allowed 6d. per day. The mayor gave a dinner at Christmas to all the inmates. Firing was found by the corporation throughout the building. There were seventy-one debtors and thirty-nine felons confined on the occasion of our visit. In one of the Towers there were seven rooms allotted to debtors, and three in another tower, in what was called "the masters side." The poorer debtors were allowed loose straw to lie upon. Those who could afford to do so, paid ls. per week for the use of a bed provided by the gaoler. The detaining creditor of debtors had to pay "groating money," that is to say, 4d. per day for their maintenance. In the chapel there was a gallery, close to which were five sleeping-rooms for male debtors. The size of these cells was six feet by seven. Over the Pilot Office in Water-street were two rooms appropriated to the use of female debtors. One of these rooms contained three beds, the other only one. This latter room had glazed windows, and a fire-place, and was, comparatively speaking, comfortable. The same charge was made for the beds in these rooms as in other parts of the prison. The debtors were also accommodated with rooms in a house adjoining the gaol, from which, by the way, an escape of many of the prisoners, felon and debtor, took place in 1807—a circumstance which created immense public interest. When the prisoners were discovered, they stood at bay, and it was not until they were fired upon, that they surrendered. The criminals were lodged in seven close dungeons 6½ feet by 5 feet 9 inches. These cells were ranged in a passage 11 feet wide, under ground, and were approached by ten steps. Over each cell door was an aperture which admitted such light and air as could be found in such a place. Some improvement took place in this respect after Mr. Howard's visit. There was also a large dungeon or cell which looked upon the street, in which twelve prisoners were confined. This dungeon was not considered safe, so that only deserters were put into it. As many as forty persons have been incarcerated in it at one time. In five of the cells there were four prisoners; in the other two, there were only three.

The court-yards (one of which was 20 yards by 30, the other 20 yards by 10) were kept in a most filthy state, although a fine pump of good water was readily accessible. The yards were brick-paved. In one yard I noticed a large dung-heap, which, I was informed, was only removed once a month. There were numbers of fowls about the yard, belonging to the prison officials and to the prisoners. In these yards, as may readily be supposed, scenes of great disorder took place. The utmost licentiousness was prevalent in the prison throughout. Spirits and malt liquors were freely introduced without let, hindrance, or concealment, though against the prison rules— not one of which, by the way, (except the feeing portion) was kept. The felons' "garnish," as it was called, was abolished previous to 1809, but the debtors' fee remained. The prison was dirty in the extreme; the mud almost ankle deep in some parts in the passages, and the walls black and grimy. There seemed to be no system whatever tending towards cleanliness, and as to health that was utterly disregarded. Low typhoid fever was frequently prevalent, and numbers were swept off by it. The strong prisoners used to tyrannise over the weak, and the most frightful cases of extortion and cruelty were practised amongst them, while the conduct of the officials was culpable in the highest degree. At one time the chapel was let as an assembly room. The prisoners used to get up, on public ball nights, dances of their own, as the band could be plainly heard throughout the prison. The debtors used to let down a glove or bag by means of a stick, from their tower into the street, dangling it up and down to attract the notice of passengers, who dropped in pieces of money for the use of the "poor debtors," which money was invariably spent in feasting and debauchery. The town boys used to put stones into the bags, and highly relished the disappointment of the "poor debtors," on discovery of their "treasure."

I recollect an execution taking place in front of the Tower, which created an immense sensation throughout the country. In March 1789, two men named Burns and Dowling, suffered the extreme penalty of the law for robbing the house of Mrs. Graham, which stood on Rose Hill. They broke into the lady's dwelling, and acted with great ferocity. It was on the 23rd December previous; they entered the house, with two others, about seven o'clock in the morning. One stayed below, while the others went into the different rooms armed with pistols and knives, threatening the various members of the family with death if they made any alarm. They robbed some guests in the house of nineteen guineas, and some silver; and from Mrs. Graham they took bills to a large amount. On the 7th January, following, Burns and Dowling were arrested at Bristol, in consequence of an anonymous letter sent to the mayor of that city, giving information of their being in the neighbourhood. They were on the point of embarking for Dublin, having several packages containing Mrs. Graham's property on board the vessel, besides £1000 in Bills of Exchange. Dowling made a fierce resistance, and would have escaped, but was held by the leg by a dog belonging to one of the constables. Rose Hill at that time was quite in the suburbs, and was a very fashionable locality. The town was crowded with strangers from all parts to witness the execution of these villains. Men of the present day would be horror-struck at the number of executions that took place at that time in England. I recollect once when in London (I was only three days going there) seeing three men hanging at Newgate, while the coal waggoners were letting off their waggons as stages for spectators at twopence per head.

The various prisoners in the Tower were all removed to the new gaol, or French prison, as it was called, on the French being released from custody, at the peace of 1812. This prison, which stood in Great Howard-street—I little thought I should live to see it swept away—was designed by Mr. Howard. Great Howard-street was called after him. The Frenchmen did so much damage to the gaol, that it cost £2000 to put it in order after their departure. These people maintained themselves by making fancy articles, and carved bone and ivory work. I once saw a ship made by one of them—an exquisite specimen of ingenuity and craftsmanship. The ropes, which were all spun to the proper sizes, were made of the prisoner's wife's hair. I had in my possession for many years, two cabinets, with drawers, &c., made of straw, and most beautifully inlaid.

I went with Mr. Nield, in one of his visits to Liverpool, to inspect the Bridewell which stood on the Fort. The building was intended for a powder magazine; but being found damp, it was not long used for that purpose. The keeper was Robert Walton, who was paid one guinea per week wages. There were no perquisites attached to this place, neither in "fees" nor "garnish." In fact, the prisoners confined within its dreary, damp walls had nothing to pay for, nor expect. There were no accommodations of any sort. The corporation certainly found "firing," but nothing else, either in beds or food, not even water. There was no yard to it, nor convenience of any kind. Under ground were two dreary, damp, dark vaults, approached by eight steps. One of them was 18 feet by 12, the other 12 feet by 7½. They received little light through iron-barred windows. Above were two rooms. One was 18 feet by 10, the other 10 feet by 9. Adjoining these two rooms, devoid of fire-grate or windows, were two cells, each 5 feet by 6 feet high. The prisoners in this dreadful place, were herded together, unemployed in any way, and dependent entirely upon their friends for food. It was a disgrace to humanity. It was damp, dirty, and in a most miserable condition.

An interesting circumstance connected with the Tower I find detailed in a book of my father's, which he called "*The Family Log.*" It relates to the escape of some prisoners-of-war confined in the Tower. My father in this "Log," used to enter up at the week's end any little circumstance of interest that might have come under his notice. At the date of Sunday, *May 6th,* 1759, I find "That fifteen French prisoners escaped from the Tower, Durand amongst the number"; and then follows a narrative which I shall presently transcribe. I may say, incidentally, that the prisoners-of-war in the Tower were principally Frenchmen, who had been captured during some of our naval engagements with them. They employed their time in making many curious and tasteful articles, and displayed great ingenuity in many ways. Discipline in the Tower was not very stringent, so that escapes of prisoners frequently occurred. From the want of energy displayed by the authorities in recapturing those that did escape, it was thought that government was not sorry to get rid of some of these persons at so easy a rate, for they were a great burden on the nation. The reason why Durand's name was mentioned as one of those who had fled, was this:—my mother had a very curiously-constructed foreign box, which had been broken, and which the tradesmen in the town had one and all declined even to attempt to repair. As "the Frenchmen" in the Tower were noted for their ingenuity, my father made some inquiry as to whether any of them would undertake the restoration of this box. Amongst others to whom it was shown was one Felix Durand, who at once said he would try to put it in order if my father was in no hurry for it, as it would be a tedious task in consequence of having so many separate pieces to join together, and it would be necessary to wait the fast binding of each cemented piece to its corresponding fragment.

My father often went to see Durand, and was much pleased with his conversation, amusing stories, and natural abilities. My father spoke French well, so that they got on capitally together, and the consequence was that my father obtained several little favours for him, and even interceded with some friends in the government to obtain his release. Durand knew of this, and, therefore, when my father found he had escaped with the others, he was much annoyed as it completely frustrated his good intentions towards him. My father used to tell us that according to agreement he went for his box on a certain day when it was to be finished. On reaching the gaol he was told of the escape of the party, and that some of them had already been recaptured. It seems that as soon as they got into the street the party dispersed, either singly or in twos and threes; but having neither food nor money, and being quite ignorant of the English language or the localities round Liverpool, they were quite helpless and everywhere betrayed who they were, what they were, and where they came from. Some fell in with the town watchmen; others struck out into the country, and after wandering about in a starved, hungry, and miserable state, were very glad to get back to their old shelter, bad as they thought it, and hardly as they considered they had been treated. They admitted that their party was too large, that they had no friends to co-operate with them outside, and no plan of action which was possibly or likely to be carried out successfully. The lot of these, however, was not shared by all, for Durand, as will be seen by his recital, had not done amiss, thanks to his wit, ingenuity, and cleverness.

The following is Durand's narrative:—

"As you know, Monsieur Le Capitaine (he always called my father so), I am a Frenchman, fond of liberty and change, and this detestable prison became so very irksome to me, with its scanty food and straw beds on the floor, that I had for some time determined to make my escape and go to Ireland, where I believe sympathies are strong towards the French nation. I am, as you know, acquainted with Monsieur P---, who resides in Dale-street; I have done some work for him. He has a niece who is *toute a faite charmante*. She has been a constant ambassador between us, and has brought me work frequently, and taken charge of my money when I have received any, to deposit with her uncle on my account. I hold that young lady in the highest consideration. This place is bad for anyone to have property in, although we are in misery alike. Some of us do not know the difference between my own and thy own. We have strange communist ideas in this building. Now "Monsieur Le Capitaine" you want to know how I got away, where I went, and how I came back. I will tell you. I could not help it. I have had a pleasing three months' holiday, and must be content to wait for peace or death, to release me from this *sacre* place. The niece of Monsieur P--- is very engaging, and when I have had conversation with her in the hall where we are permitted to see our friends, I obtained from her the information that on the east side of our prison there were two houses which opened into a short narrow street. One of these houses had been lately only partly tenanted, while the lower portion of it had been under repair. Mademoiselle is very complacent and kind. She took the trouble to go for me to the house and examine it, and reported that there was an open yard under the eastern prison-wall, and if anybody could get through that wall he might easily continue his route through the house and into the street. My mind was soon made up. I imparted my intention to my companions. There were fifteen of us, altogether, penned up at night in a vile cell or vault, and, of course, the intended escape could not be kept a secret; what was known by one, must be known by all. We all resolved to escape. Our cell was dirty and miserable. We obtained light and air from the street as well as from a grating over the door. Choosing a somewhat stormy night, we commenced by loosening the stonework in the east wall. Now we knew that after we were locked up for the night we should not be disturbed, and if we could not effect the removal of the stones in one night, there would be no fear of discovery during the next day, as we were seldom molested by any of the gaolers. We could walk about the prison just as we liked and mix with the other prisoners, whether felons or debtors. In fact your Liverpool Tower contains a large family party. We worked all night at the wall, and just before daybreak contrived to remove a large stone and soon succeeded in displacing another, but light having at length broken, we gathered up all the mortar and rubbish we had made, stuffing some of it into our beds, and covering the rest with them in the best way we could. To aid us in preventing the gaoler discovering what we had been about, one of our party remained in bed when the doors were unlocked, and we curtained the window grating with a blanket, stating that our *compatriote* was very ill and that he could not bear the light. We had no dread of a doctor coming to visit him, for unless special application was made for medical attendance on the sick nobody seemed to care whether we lived or died. The day passed over without any suspicions arising from our preparations. The afternoon set in stormy, as the preceding evening had done, and in the course of the night of our escape we had a complete hurricane of rain and wind, which eventually greatly favoured us by clearing the streets of any stragglers who might be prowling about. No sooner were we locked in at night than we recommenced our work at the wall, and were not long in making a hole sufficient to allow a man to creep through, which one of us did. He reported himself to be in an open yard, that it was raining very heavily, and that the night was *affreuse;* we all then crept through. We found ourselves in a dark yard, with a house before us. We obtained a light in a shed on one side of the yard, and then looked about. We found a sort of cellar door by the side of a window. We tried to open it: to our surprise it yielded. Screening our light we proceeded into a passage, taking off our shoes and stockings first (some of us had none to take off, poor fellows!) so that we should make no noise. The house was quite still; we scarcely dared to breathe. We went forward and entered a kitchen in which were the remains of a supper. We took possession of all that was eatable on the table. It was wonderful that nobody heard us, for one of us let fall a knife after cutting up a piece of beef into pieces, so that each man might have a share. Although there were people in the house no one heard us; truly you Englishmen sleep well! Before us was a door—we opened it. It was only a closet. We next thought of the window, for we dared not climb up stairs to the principal entrance. We tried the shutters which we easily took down and, fortunately without noise, opened the window, through which one of us crept to reconnoitre. He was only absent about a minute or two, returning to tell us that not a soul was to be seen anywhere; that the wind was rushing up the main street from the sea, and that the rain was coming down in absolute torrents. Just as the neighbouring church clock struck two we were assembled under an archway together. We determined to disperse, and let every man take care of himself. Bidding my friends good bye I struck out into the street. At first I thought of going to the river, but suddenly decided to go inland. I therefore went straight on, passed the Exchange, and down a narrow street facing it (Dale-street) in which I knew mademoiselle dwelt. I thought of her, but had no hope of seeing her as I did not know the house wherein she resided. I pushed on, therefore, until I came to the foot of a hill; I thought I would turn to the left, but shutting my eyes with superstitious feelings I left myself to fate, and determined to go forward with my eyes closed until I had by chance selected one of the four cross roads [Old Haymarket, Townsend-lane (now Byrom-street), Dale-street, and Shaw's-brow] which presented themselves for my choice.

"I soon found I was ascending a hill, and on opening my eyes I discovered that I was pursuing my route in an easterly direction. I passed up a narrow street with low dirty-looking houses on each side, and from the broken mugs and earthenware my feet encountered in the darkness, I felt sure I was passing through the outskirts of Liverpool—famous for its earthenware manufactures. During all this time I had not seen a living thing; in fact it was scarcely possible for anything to withstand the storm that raged so vehemently. In this, however, rested my safety. I sped on, and soon mounting the hill paused by the side of a large windmill (Townsend mill) which stood at the top of London-road. Having gained breath, I pushed forward, taking the road to the right hand which ran before me (then called the road to Prescot). I began now to breathe freely and feel some hope in my endeavour to escape. My limbs, which, from long confinement in prison, were stiff at first, now felt elastic and nimble and I pushed on at a quick pace, the wind blowing at my back the whole time; still onward I went until I got into a country lane and had another steep hill to mount. The roads were very heavy. The sidewalk was badly kept, and the rain made it ankle-deep with mud. On surmounting the hill, which I afterwards learned was called Edge-hill, I still kept on to the right hand road, which was lined on both sides with high trees. I at length arrived at a little village (Wavertree) as a clock was striking three; still not a soul was visible. I might have been passing through a world of the dead. After traversing this village I saw, on my left hand, a large pond, at which I drew some water in my cap. I was completely parched with my unusual exertions. Resting under a large tree which proved some shelter, I ate up the bread and meat I had procured from the kitchen of the house through which we had escaped. Having rested about half-an-hour I again started forward. I now began to turn over in my mind what I should do. I felt that if I could get to Ireland I could find friends who would assist me. I knew a French priest in Dublin on whom I could rely for some aid. I at length hit upon a course of action which I determined to pursue. Through narrow lanes I went, still keeping to the right, and after walking for more than an hour I found myself in a quaint little village (Hale) in which there was a church then building. The houses were constructed principally of timber, lath, and plaster and were apparently of great antiquity. Onward still I went, the rain beating down heavily and the wind blowing. In about a quarter of an hour I gained a sight of the river or the sea, I know not which, but I still continued my road until I came up to a little cottage, the door of which opened just as I was passing it. An old woman came out and began to take down the shutters. Now, as I came along the road I had made up my mind to personate a deaf and dumb person, which would preclude the necessity of my speaking. I felt I could do this well and successfully. I determined to try the experiment upon this old lady. I walked quietly up to her, took the shutters out of her hands and laid them in their proper places. I then took a broom and began sweeping away the water which had accumulated in front of her cottage, and seeing a kettle inside the door, I walked gravely into the house, took it, and filled it at a pump close by. The old woman was dumb-struck. Not a word did she say, but stood looking on with mute amazement, which was still more intensely exhibited when I went to the fire-place, raked out the cinders, took up some sticks and commenced making a fire. Not a word passed between us. It was with great difficulty I could keep my countenance. We must have looked a curious couple. The woman standing staring at me, I sitting on a three-legged stool, with my elbows on my knees looking steadfastly at her. At length she broke this unnatural silence. Speaking in her broad Lancashire dialect I could scarcely make her out. My own deficiency in not understanding much English increased my difficulty, but I understood her to ask "Who I was, and whither I was going." This she repeated until, having sufficiently excited her curiosity, I opened my mouth very wide, kept my tongue quite close so that it might seem as if I had none, and with my fingers to my ears made a gesture that I was deaf and dumb. She then said, "Poor man, poor man," with great feeling and gave me a welcome. So I sat before the fire, and commenced drying my clothes, which were saturated during my walk. I suppose I must have fallen asleep, for the next thing I noticed was a substantial meal laid on the table, consisting of bread, cold bacon, and beer. Pointing to the food the old woman motioned to me to partake, and this I was not loath to do. I made a hearty meal. I should tell you, before we sat down to the table I had pulled out my pockets to show her I had no money. The woman made a sign that she did not want payment for her kindness. When we had finished our meal I looked about me, and seeing that several things wanted putting to rights, such as emptying a bucket, getting in some coals, and cleaning down the front pavement of the house, I commenced working hard as some repayment for the hospitality I had received. We Frenchmen can turn our hands to almost anything, and my dexterity quite pleased the old lady. While I was busily sweeping the hearth, I heard the sound of a horse's feet coming swiftly onward. Terror-struck, I did a foolish thing. Fancying it must be some one in pursuit of me, I dropped the little broom I was using, seized my cap from one of the chairs, opened the back door of the cottage, and fled along the garden walk, over-leaped a hedge, crossed a brook, and was off like a hunted hare across the open fields. This was a silly proceeding, because if the horseman had been any one in pursuit, the chances were that, should he have entered the cottage, I might not have been recognized; and if I had simply hid myself in some of the outbuildings that were near I might have escaped notice altogether, while by running across the fields I exposed myself to observation, and to be taken. When half over a field I found there a small clump of trees, and a little pond. Down the side of this pond I slipped and hid myself amongst the rushes; but I need not have given myself any anxiety or trouble, for I saw the horseman, whatever might have been his errand, flying along the winding road in the distance.

"Having satisfied myself of my security, I started off and soon found myself on the highroad again, and after a time I came near a fine old mansion which presented a most venerable appearance. I could not stop, however, to look at it, for I found I had taken a wrong turn and was going back to Liverpool. I therefore retraced my steps and passed on, going I know not whither. After walking for about an hour in a southerly direction, feeling tired and seeing a barn open I went to it and found two men therein threshing wheat. I made signs to them that I was deaf and dumb, and asked leave to lie in the straw. They stared at me very much, whispered amongst themselves, and at length, made a sign of assent. I fell asleep. When I awoke the sun was up and bright, while all trace of the night-storm had disappeared. I wondered at first where I was. Seeing the fresh straw lying about, an idea struck me that I could earn a few pence by a little handiwork. I thereupon commenced making some straw baskets, the like of which you have often seen myself and fellow-prisoners manufacture. By the time I had completed two or three the men came again into the barn and began to work with their flails. I stepped forward with my baskets, which seemed to surprise them. The like they had evidently never seen before—they examined them with the greatest attention. One of the men, pulling some copper money out of his pocket, offered it for one of them. Grateful for the shelter I had received, I pushed back the man's hand which contained the money and offered him the basket as a present, pointing to my bed of straw. The honest fellow would not accept it, saying I must have his money. I therefore sold him one of the baskets, and another was also purchased by one of the other men. They seemed astonishingly pleased with their bargains. Just as they had concluded their dealings with me a big man came into the barn, who I found out was the master. The men showed him the baskets and pointed to me, telling the farmer that I was a "dumby and deafy." The big farmer hereupon bawled in my ear the question, "who was I, and where had I come from?" I put on a perfectly stolid look although the drum of my ears was almost split by his roaring. The farmer had a soft heart, however, in his big and burly frame. Leaving the barn, he beckoned me to follow him. This I did. He went into the farm-house, and, calling his wife, bade her get dinner ready. A capital piece of beef, bread, and boiled greens or cabbages were soon on the table, to which I sat down with the farmer and his wife. Their daughter, soon after we had commenced eating, came in. Her attention was immediately attracted by my remaining basket, which I had placed by them. I got up from the table and presented it to her. Her father then told her of my supposed infirmities. I could scarcely help laughing while I heard them canvass my personal appearance, my merits and demerits. Pity, however, seemed to be the predominant feeling. When the dinner was over, I happened to look up at an old clock and saw that it had stopped. I went up to it, and took it from the nail. I saw it wanted but very little to make it go again. I therefore quietly, but without taking notice of my companions, set to work to take off the face and do the needful repairs. A pair of pincers on the window-ledge and some iron wire, in fact, an old skewer, were all the tools necessary; and very soon, to the satisfaction of my host, his wife, and his fair daughter, the clock was set going as well as it ever had done. The farmer slapped me on the back and gave me great encouragement. I then cast my eyes about to see what I could do next. I mended a chair, repaired a china image, cleaned an old picture, and taking a lock from a door repaired it, altering the key so that it became useful. In fact, I so busied myself, and with such earnestness that by night-time I had done the farmer a good pound's worth of repairing. I then had my supper, and was made to understand I might sleep in the barn, if I liked. On the next morning the farmer's daughter found me very busy in the yard with the pigs, which I was feeding; in fact, the whole of that day I worked hard, because I thought if I could remain where I was until the wonder of our escapade was over, I might eventually get away altogether from England by some unforeseen piece of good fortune. For some time I worked at this farm, for, as if by mutual consent of the farmer and myself, I remained, getting only my food for my work; however, at the end of each week the farmer's wife gave me quietly some money. I made several little fancy articles for Mademoiselle which she seemed highly to prize; but it was through her that I left my snug quarters. The principal labourer on the farm was courting, on the sly, this young woman, and I noticed he became sulky with me, as Miss Mary on several occasions selected me to perform some little service for her. From an expression I heard him make use of to one of the other men I felt sure he was about to do me some act of treachery and unkindness, and, as I was no match for the great Hercules he seemed to be, I thought it best to leave the place, as any disturbance might draw down attention upon me too closely. I therefore put up my spare clothes, some of which had been given to me by the farmer's wife—a kindly, Christian woman she was—and hiding my little store of money securely in my breeches' waistband, very early one fine morning I set off with a heart by no means light, from the place where I had been so well-treated, not knowing where on earth to go or what next to do. Before I went, however, to show I was grateful for their kindness, I made up a little parcel which I addressed to the farmer's wife, in which I put a tobacco-box for Mr. John Bull, a bodkin-case for herself, and a little ring for Miss Mary, all of which I had made in my leisure time. I dare say they were sorry to part with me. I am sure Miss Mary was, for I fancied she suspected I was not what I seemed, and had begun to take an evident liking to me. I had taught her some French modes of cooking, which excited surprise, as well as gratification to their palates, and I taught her also two or three little ways of making fancy articles that pleased her exceedingly. It was through her manifesting a preference for me that, as I have told you, Monsieur le Capitaine, I felt obliged to absent myself from her father's employment. It was most difficult at first to restrain myself from talking. But I soon got over that, for when I was about to speak I made an uncertain sort of noise, which turned off suspicion. That the head labourer had some doubt about me, I verily believe. I thought at first I would try to get to London, but the roads thereto, I learnt, were so bad and travelling so insecure, even for the poorest, that I considered it best to remain in this neighbourhood, as I wanted to see Mademoiselle P--- once more, and settle with her uncle for the money of mine in his hands. I thought if I could only communicate with him he would befriend me, so I went on my way.

"I travelled all that day until I got into a place called Warrington, by the side of a river. It is a town full of old quaint houses built of timber and plaster. I was very tired when I arrived there at nightfall, but obtained shelter in an old house near the bridge, and as I had the money my mistress gave me I bought some food at a little shop; a Frenchman does not want very heavy meals, so that I did pretty well. The next day I went to a baker's and got some more bread. I interested the baker's wife, and when she found I was deaf and dumb, she not only would not take money for her bread, but also gave me some meat and potatoes. It seemed she had a relation affected as I was supposed to be. I then went out to a farm-yard, and having begged some straw I turned to my never-failing fountain of help—basket making. I made a number of baskets and other little things, all of which on taking into the town I sold readily. I begged some more straw of a man at a stable, and set to work again. I sold off my baskets and fancy articles much quicker than I could make them. I soon got so well known that I excited some attention; but one day being at a public tavern, where I had gone to deliver a basket ordered, the word 'Liverpool' fell upon my ears and caused me to tremble. Near me sat two men who looked like drovers. They were talking about Liverpool affairs: one of them told the other that there had been lately a great fire near the dock, where a quantity of provisions had been burnt, and much property destroyed besides. They then spoke of the escape of my companions and myself, and for the first time I heard of their fate, and how, one by one, they had been recaptured or willingly returned. I then heard of their trials and the miseries they had encountered. The drovers also spoke of one prisoner who had disappeared and got away completely, but that there was a hot search after him, as he, it was supposed, was the ringleader in the late outbreak, and that it was planned and carried out by him. I felt that they alluded to myself, and that this place would grow too warm for me, as I knew that I was already an object of public remark, owing to my supposed infirmities and the extraordinary dexterity of my fingers. It will be recollected that I bought some bread at a little shop near the market-place. Passing there the day after I arrived, I saw a bill in the window bearing the words *"lodgings to let."* I, therefore, by signs made the woman of the shop comprehend that I wanted such accommodation. I took the bill out of the window, pointed to the words, and the to myself; then I laid my hand on my head as if in the attitude of sleep. The good woman quite comprehended me, and nodding her head to my dumb proposition led the way up a small flight of stairs, and at once installed me in the vacant room. It was small and poorly furnished, but very clean. I soon made myself at home; and never wanted anything doing for me, so that the widow's intercourse with me was very limited. I knew I could not write without betraying my foreign origin, so the way I did first was to get a book and pick out words signifying what I wanted, and from these words the good woman made out a sentence. I wanted so little that we had no difficulty in making out a dialogue. After hearing the talk of the drovers I determined to leave the town without delay, for my fears of recapture quite unmanned me, making me needlessly dread any intercourse with strangers. Having thus resolved to leave Warrington I bade goodbye to my kind landlady, giving her a trifle over her demand, and then shaped my way to the northward. I went to several towns, large and small, and stayed in Manchester a week, where I sold what I made very readily. My supposed infirmities excited general commiseration everywhere, and numerous little acts of kindness did I receive. I wandered about the neighbouring towns in the vicinity for a long time, being loth to leave it for several reasons; in fact I quite established a connection amongst the farmers and gentry, who employed me in fabricating little articles of fancy work and repairing all sorts of things most diverse in their natures and uses. At one farm-house I mended a tea-pot and a ploughshare, and at a gentleman's house, near St. Helen's, repaired a cart, and almost re-built a boat, which was used on his fish-pond. I turned my hand to any and everything. I do not say I did everything well, but I did it satisfactorily to those who employed me. I now began to be troubled about my money which was accumulating, being obliged to carry it about with me, as I feared being pillaged of it. I therefore resolved on coming back to Liverpool and finding out Monsieur P--- at all hazards, trusting to chance that I should not be recognised. Who could do so? Who would know me in the town save the Tower gaolers who would scarcely be out at night; even they would not recollect me in the dark streets of the town? When this resolve came upon me I was at a place called Upholland where I had been living three or four days, repairing some weaver's looms—for there are a good many weavers in that little town. I had nearly finished the work I had undertaken, and was intending to come to Liverpool direct at the end of the following week, when my design was frustrated by a curious and most unexpected circumstance. About three miles from Upholland there is a very high hill called Ashurst. On the top of this is a beacon tower which looks at a distance like a church steeple rising over the top of the hill, just as if the body of the church were on the other side of the crest. This beacon is intended to communicate alarm to the neighbouring country in war time, it being one of a line of beacons to and from different places. I had once or twice walked to this high place to enjoy the fine prospect. On Sunday last I had gone there and extended my walk down the hill to a place where the road, after passing a pretty old entrance-gateway, moat, and old hall, dips very prettily down to bridge over a small stream. This bridge (Cobb's Brow Bridge) is covered with ivy, and is very picturesque. Just before the road rather abruptly descends there are, on the right hand side of it, a number of remarkably old and noble oak trees, quite giants. Some are hollowed out, and one is so large that it will accommodate several persons. This tree has been used by what you call gipsies—and shows that fire has been made in it.

"Well, on Sunday, in the afternoon, I was sitting under one of these fine old trees, when I saw a cavalcade coming down the road, consisting of two ladies and a gentleman mounted on fine horses, and attended by two serving-men or grooms. When the party had arrived opposite the trees they stopped to examine them, when one of the ladies, struck with the wonderful size of the largest tree, expressed her admiration of it in very purely-pronounced French. I was so surprised that I became completely unnerved, was thrown off my guard, and, in the excitement of the moment, at hearing my native tongue so beautifully pronounced, sprang up, and rushing forward echoed in my own tongue the lady's commendation of those grand old trees. I immediately found out my error, for, to my grief, the other young lady, whom I at once recognized, exclaimed—"Why this is the dumb man who was at the Hall the other day repairing the broken glass vases!" I at first denied that such was the case, but on the grooms coming up they both identified me. In fact, I knew both from having applied to the younger of the two, only a few days previously, to obtain for me employment in the house of his master, in any way my services could be made available. Thus I had through him obtained permission to repair the vases which had been much injured, and which I had most successfully put in order. The gentleman then asked me who I was, called me an impostor, and ordered his servants to seize me. This they did, when I at once admitted who I was and where I came from. The gentleman, although entreated most earnestly by the ladies to allow me to go away, would not consent to his servants releasing me, but ordered them to take me to Ormschurch (Ormskirk), about five miles distant, and have me put into the little prison there, which you call the cage. The ladies, with tears in their eyes, on seeing me thus seized by the servant-men, bade them not use me roughly, and one of them slipped a gold piece into my hand, bidding me in French to be of good cheer, for there was a talk of immediate peace, when I should be released. The gentleman rode away calling the young ladies to follow him without delay, bidding, at the same time, the servants to see that I was delivered over to the proper authorities at Ormschurch, so that I might be transmitted to Liverpool. As soon as the master and the ladies were out of sight, one of the men, who rode a stout horse, bade me get up behind him, which I did, and in about an hour we arrived in the town. It was full of people in their Sunday clothes. My appearance attracted some notice, I was pitied by some, execrated by others, and followed by crowds of boys. After waiting in the street some time I was taken before a stout, growling old gentleman, who ordered me to be locked up until the next morning, and to have meat and drink given me. I was then to be taken to Liverpool and delivered over to my gaoler again. In accordance with this order I was put into a small square room, on the floor of which was a quantity of straw. There were benches fixed in the walls. There was no fire-place and it was sadly uncomfortable. However, soon after I was locked up, I received a good supply of bread, meat, and beer; and, as the straw was tolerably fresh and clean, I did not fare so badly. I therefore lay down, covered myself up with the straw, and was soon fast asleep. I awoke once, but as everything was dark, I composed myself to sleep again and did not awake until morning. About six o'clock, as I knew by the church-clock hard by, I was aroused and told to be ready to start for Liverpool, whereupon I presented myself at the door, and found an open cart in waiting. Into this I was put, and, after a tiresome journey over some of the worst roads I had ever seen in my life, I arrived here last night, having enjoyed a three months' holiday to my great satisfaction. Here, then, I am, waiting for death or peace to release me. I shall now finish your box if you are not too offended with me for neglecting your commission so long. I may tell you that Mademoiselle P--- was here this morning; tears were in her lovely eyes, and she seemed very glad to see me back, at which I somewhat wondered, especially if she esteemed me. I should have thought she would rather have relished my escaping altogether, than being again caught."

Here ends Durand's narrative.

My father appends a note to the effect that, through the intervention of Sir Edward Cunliffe, one of the members for Liverpool, Durand was released from the Tower, and went to reside with Mr. P--- in Dale-street. At the date of September following there is a memorandum to the effect that M. Durand and Miss P--- had become man and wife, so that, as my father quaintly adds, he supposes M. Durand had by that time found out why it was that old P---'s niece was so glad to see him again in prison.

The House of Correction stood at the back of the present Fever Hospital, the entrance being in Mount Pleasant. It was in Mr. Howard's time a most miserably managed place. In 1790 it was a vile hole of iniquity. There was a whipping-post, for instance, in the yard, at which females were weekly in the receipt of punishment. There was also "a cuckstool," or ducking tub, where refractory prisoners were brought to their senses, and in which persons on their first admission into the gaol were ducked, if they refused or could not pay "a garnish." This barbarous mode of punishment was common in Lancashire, and Cheshire. This prison was in the course of the following years much improved, as it was found by Mr. Neild very clean and orderly through the exertions of Mrs. Widdows, the keeper. Mrs. Widdow's salary was £63 per annum. She had resolutely put down the cuckstool, and the whipping-post was becoming in a complete state of desuetude. A pump in the men's yard was used as a place of occasional punishment for the stubborn and refractory. The prisoners were without any instruction, secular or religious. No chaplain attended. The allowance to each prisoner was a two-penny loaf, two pounds of potatoes, and salt daily. I believe, from all I could learn, that the Liverpool prisons, bad as they undoubtedly were at the close of the last and the beginning of the present century, were in better condition than others elsewhere.

# CHAPTER III.

One of my great-grandsons—a fine young fellow, has joined the Volunteers: and seems determined to work his way to a commission. I cannot help smiling when I see him in his uniform, for he reminds me of my young days, when I was a full private in Pudsey Dawson's Liverpool Volunteers. I don't think the volunteers of this day are so smart-looking as they were of olden time, when they wore blue coats, white breeches, gaiters and pig-tails, and used pipe-clay in abundance. When we were reviewed on Moss-Lake Fields we made a gallant show. There are fine young fellows now, but somehow the dark rifle-dress looks sombre and dull. Pudsey Dawson's regiment consisted of eight companies of infantry, and mustered 1200 strong.

The mettle of the Liverpool men was shown in 1797, for some time about the end of February or the beginning of March, in that year the whole town was put into the utmost fright, confusion and excitement. Two French frigates having landed in Cardigan Bay upwards of 2,000 men, it was reported in Liverpool (the report being traced to the master of a little Welsh coasting smack, who had come from Cardigan) that the French were marching on to Liverpool to burn, sack and plunder it, in revenge for the frigates which had been launched from her yards, and the immense losses sustained by the French mercantile marine through the privateers that hailed from this port. Owing to the low state of education then prevalent amongst the lower— and, indeed, in the middle classes—very few knew where Cardigan Bay was situated and I very much question whether, if a map of Europe, or of England and Wales, had been shown, nine people out of ten could, without much difficulty, have pointed out the place. But that the French had landed in Cardigan Bay was a known fact; and it was firmly believed that they were on their way to Liverpool, destroying every thing on their march. It was fully believed also that the privateers which swarmed out of our docks were the cause of this exhibition of ill-feeling towards us. It may be fairly stated that the enormous sums obtained by captures from the enemy by Liverpool privateers proved the main foundation-stone of the present great prosperity of the port. I must say I was and am proud of my fellow townsmen's spirit in '97, and their show of pluck. No sooner was the report current that the French might be expected, than meetings took place at which his Worship the Mayor and the authorities generally, exhibited the most lively feeling towards supporting their fellow citizens in their intention of defending the port, their homes, and hearths, from the ruthless invaders. Men, money, and arms, came forth freely, and even boys—mere lads—urgently begged to be allowed to join the ranks of England's bold defenders. But I must not conceal the fact that, in many cases, great cowardice was exhibited; as, when the report got current and the cry was rife that "the French were coming"—a cry that used to frighten naughty children to the verge of terror—numbers of the inhabitants became panic-struck, and actually packed up their furniture and valuables, and commenced a hasty exodus believing that they would be safer inland than by the seaboard. I saw cartload after cartload of goods, toiling up Prescot-road, Brownlow-hill, Mount Pleasant, Oldhall-street, and Preston-road, accompanied by weeping and terrified women and children, with the deepest anxiety exhibited on their countenances. The outskirt roads were like a fair. It will scarcely be believed that the price of cartage rose so high while the panic lasted, that fabulous sums were asked and obtained for transporting goods out of town. It at length became impossible to obtain a vehicle of any description. Hundreds of persons might be seen camping along the high roads at some distance from the town, anxiously awaiting the expected sound of cannon, the clash of arms, and the cry of contending men. I laugh at this now—but it was no laughing matter then. I recollect one day passing down Dale-street (then a narrow, inconvenient thoroughfare) to muster, when the Warrington and Manchester coach was about to start: numbers of frightened people besieged it and attempted to turn out and off those who had obtained possession of its lumbering inside and its miserable basket behind. In it I remember was seated a tremendous man, a town councillor, who fairly roared and cried like a child because the driver would not hasten his departure—the cry of "the French" annihilated him, and I had half a mind to let off my fire-lock and see what the result would have been. We were not much addicted to punctuality in those good old times; so that half an hour's delay in the starting of a coach was held as nothing very important—the delay however seemed a year to the worthy magnate.

In the town the utmost excitement prevailed. At the Pier Heads, at the Fort, and in St. Nicholas's churchyard (in the lower part of which there was a battery of six guns) might have been seen hundreds of stalwart fellows strengthening the fortifications; men in and out of uniform were marching through the town with drum and fife, some armed and some unarmed, coming and going from or to the rendezvous. The jolly sailors in the port mustered strong, and hearty were their demonstrations of enthusiasm. The shops were shut in many of the streets, while barricades were prepared at the street ends leading out of town, ready to be put up at any moment. Information was then so slow in its journeyings that falsehood became as strong-looking as truth, and it was easy to keep up a ferment for some time. Any atom of news became a mountain, until the fresh air of truth melted it away. We were therefore kept for days in a state of great excitement, and it certainly was some time before our warlike spirit subsided, and I must say that although we were somewhat laughed at for our extraordinary haste in coming to the conclusions we did, we had nothing to be ashamed of. We Liverpool men showed our pluck on that and many other occasions during the French war. I fear we were a little too much alive. We had too much pugnacity about us if anything. I recollect some poor simple looking French fishermen in that year put into Liverpool, in order to sell some oysters, when it was all once taken for granted that they were spies, sent to ascertain what we were doing. The mayor at a meeting held to consider the state of the harbour-defences, actually alluded to these poor fishermen as having in their possession the soundings and bearings of the harbour and river-entrance. I, for one, did not believe in their being spies, never having seen such a lot of harmless, stupid-looking men.

About this period the press-gang was very actively engaged in taking men for the navy. These gangs were made up of the very worst and most violent men in the service. They were by no means particular whom they took: to them a man was a man, and that was a sufficient reason for securing him. Cases of horrible cruelty and great hardship frequently occurred to individuals. Men were constantly torn from their homes, wives, and families, without a moment's warning. They disappeared and were not heard of for years, or perhaps not at all. There was a man I knew who was seized in Pool-lane and hurried off to the tender, and was not heard of for four years, when he returned suddenly as his wife was about to be married for the third time since his departure. His arrival, with a good store of pay, and prize-money, was ample compensation for the loss of the new husband. Terrible rows took place between the press-gangs and the sailor-men—the latter resisted to the very death any attempt to capture them. Blood was frequently shed, and loss of life was not uncommon. I recollect one murderous business with which I should have been mixed up if I had not made my escape by running into a house in Atherton-street. The men used to get across the water to Cheshire to hide until their ships were ready to sail. Near Egremont, on the shore, there used to be a little low public-house, known as "Mother Redcap's," from the fact of the owner always wearing a red hood or cap. This public-house is still standing. I have often been in it. At that time there were no inner walls to divide the room on the upper floor; but only a few screens put up of about seven or eight feet in height to form apartments. The roof was not latted or plastered. When I last saw it, some twenty-five years or more ago, the joists and timbers were all open to view. Mother Redcap was a great favourite with the sailor-men and had their entire confidence. She had hiding-places for any number, and the men used, on returning from their voyages, to deposit with her their pay and prize-money, until they wanted it. It was known, or at least, very commonly believed, that Mother Redcap had in her possession enormous (for her) sums of money, hidden or put away somewhere; but where that somewhere was, it was never known; for, at her death, very little property was found in her possession, although only a few days before she was taken ill and died, a rich prize was brought into Liverpool which yielded every sailor on board at least a thousand pounds. Mother Redcap's was swarming with sailors belonging to the privateer, directly after the vessel had come into port, and it was known that the old lady had received a good deal of the prize-money on their account, yet none of it was ever discovered. It is a very remarkable circumstance that some few years ago, I think about ten or twelve, but I forget exactly when, a quantity of money in spade-ace guineas was found in a cavity by the shore, not far from Mother Redcap's. It has always been a firm belief with me that some day a rich harvest will be in store for somebody—a case of treasure trove like that which some years ago was known as "the Cuerdly Find." Mother Redcap's was the resort of many a rough, hard-hunted fellow, and many a strange story has been told, and scene enacted, under the old roof.

The passage of the river then and at the beginning of the last century, until steam-boats were introduced, was a complete and serious voyage, which few undertook. The boatmen used to run their boats at one time on the beach opposite the end of Water-street and ply for hire. After the piers were ran out they hooked on at the steps calling aloud, "Woodside, ahoy!" "Seacombe, ahoy!" and so on. It is a fact that thousands of Liverpool people at that time never were in Cheshire in their lives. We used to cross in open or half-decked boats, and sometimes we have been almost as many hours in crossing as we are now minutes. I recollect once wanting to go to Woodside on a stormy day, to see a man who lived in a small house between the Ferry-house and Wallasey Pool, and which, by the way, was the only house then standing thereabout. The tide was running very strong and the wind blowing hard, and, after nearly four hours hard work, we managed to land near the Rock Perch, thankful for our lives being spared. The Rock Perch was a pole with a sort of beacon or basket at the top of it, implanted in the rocks on which the lighthouse now stands. There were no houses then anywhere about what is now called New Brighton. The country was sandy and barren, and the only trees that existed grew close to the mouth of the river near the shore. There was scarcely a house between the Rock and Wallasey. Wirrall at that time and the middle of the last century was a desperate region. The inhabitants were nearly all wreckers or smugglers—they ostensibly carried on the trade and calling of fishermen, farm-labourers, and small farmers; but they were deeply saturated with the sin of covetousness, and many a fierce fire has been lighted on the Wirrall shore on stormy nights to lure the good ship on the Burbo or Hoyle Banks, there to beat, and strain, and throb, until her timbers parted, and her planks were floating in confusion on the stormy waves. Fine times, then, for the Cheshire men. On stormy days and nights, crowds might have been seen hurrying to the shore with carts, barrows, horses, asses, and oxen even, which were made to draw timber, bales, boxes, or anything that the raging waters might have cast up. Many a half-drowned sailor has had a knock on the sconce whilst trying to obtain a footing, that has sent him reeling back into the seething water, and many a house has been suddenly replenished with eatables and drinkables, and furniture and garniture, where previously bare walls and wretched accommodation only were visible. Then for smuggling—fine times the runners used to have in my young days. Scarcely a house in north Wirral that could not provide a guest with a good stiff glass of brandy or Hollands. The fishermen used to pretend to cast their nets to take the fish that then abounded on our coasts, but their fishing was of a far different sort. Formby, on this side, was a great place for smugglers and smuggling. I don't think they wrecked as the Cheshire people did—these latter were very fiends. The Formby fishermen were pretty honest and hardworking, and could always make a good living by their calling, so that the smuggling they did was nothing to be compared to their Cheshire compatriots. Strings upon strings of ponies have I seen coming along the road from Formby, laden with the finny spoil. The ponies had panniers slung over their backs, while sometimes the fisherman's wife or child, if the horse could bear the double burden, was seated between them. These were called "Formby Trotters." There were good fish caught in the river at that time; and I have heard say that herrings used to be taken in great profusion in our vicinity until the people fought at the Fish Stones by St. Nicholas's Church wall, and blood was shed on the occasion. Many a fisherman steadfastly believed that the herrings then left the coast, and never returned in consequence. Wallasey was certainly, at one period, a great place for the curing of herrings, as can be proved by tradition as well as written history.

How well I recollect the Woodside Ferry when I was a boy. There was a long causeway at it, which ran into the river, formed of logs of wood and large boulder stones. Up this causeway you walked until you came to the overhanging shore which on the left hand was cut away to admit the causeway continuing up into the land. There was a small thicket of trees on the rock-top and a patch of garden which belonged to the ferryman. The only house visible was a farm-house which stood on the spot where the (Gough's) Woodside Hotel may now be found. It had a garden enclosed by a hedge round it. The road to Bidston was a rough, rutted way, and the land was for the most part marshy between Woodside and Bidston, and the country looked very desolate, wild, and rugged. There were some pretty walks over the fields. There was one from Holt Hill to Oxton which I was very fond of. When the weather was fine I have had many and many a pleasant ramble over land where now houses show themselves in hundreds, nay, thousands, and where I have gone bird-nesting, and picking wild flowers, and mushrooming in their season. Lord! what changes I have seen and yet live to see; and I am very thankful for His mercies, which have been manifold and abundant. Wallasey Pool was a glorious piece of water once, and many a good fish I have taken out of it in the upper waters. The view of Birkenhead Priory was at one time very picturesque, before they built the church near it and the houses round it. I recollect when there was not a dwelling near it. It seemed to stand out well in the landscape, and certainly looked very pretty. It was a great shame that persons should have been permitted to carry away the stones for building or any other purpose. Had not a stop at last been put to this sort of work there would not in time have been a vestige of the old Abbey left. I recollect that there was a belief that a tunnel or subterraneous passage ran under the Mersey to Liverpool from the Priory, and that the entrance in 1818, when the church was built, had been found and a good way traversed. That passage was commonly spoken of as being in existence when I was a boy, and I often vowed I would try to find it. I have been up the tunnels or caves at the Red and White Noses many a time for great distances. I was once fishing for codling at the Perch, and with two young companions went up the caves for at least a mile, and could have gone further only we became frightened as our lights went out. It was thought these caves ran up to Chester Cathedral—but that was all stuff. I believe they were excavated by smugglers in part, and partly natural cavities of the earth. We knew little then of archaeology or geology, or any other "ology," or I might be able to tell a good deal about these caves, for I saw them more than once, but I now forget what their size and height was. The floor, I recollect, was very uneven and strewed about with big stones, while the roof was arched over in the red sand-stone. The encroachment of the sea upon the Wirral shore has been very gradual, but regular, for many years. Within the memory of man the sea has made an inroad of nearly, if not quite, a mile from its former high-water mark. It was not until the erection of the Wallasey embankment that a stop was put to its ravages.

When I stand on the Pier-head, or take my daily walk on the Landing-Stage, I often pause and revolve in my mind the wonderful changes that have taken place in my time in this native town of mine. The other day, soon after the completion of the large Landing-Stage, I sat down and thought would any man then making use of the old baths, swimming inside the palisade, have not considered me, some eighty years ago, a mad fool to have predicted that before I died I should sit on a long floating stage two or three hundred yards from where we were swimming, that would be about a quarter of a mile in length, and that between it and the shore there would be most wonderful docks built, in which the ships of all nations would display their colours, and discharge their precious freights? As I sat there the other day, I thought of the one bath and the old houses by the river's brink, and the Bath-street, along which came, in the summer-time, such strings of country "dowkers." Beyond the baths there were no houses, all was open shore consisting of boulder stones, sand, and pools, such as may be seen on any sea-beach. There was hot as well as cold water bathing in the baths, and a palisade ran out into the river, within which, at high-water, persons could swim, as in a plunge-bath. These baths were erected originally by Mr. Wright, who sold them to the corporation in 1774, by which body they were enlarged and greatly improved.

I recollect the bath-woman sold a sort of parliament cake, covered over with coloured sugar plums, and also some sweet things which in appearance resembled slugs. I never see these caraway-cakes and confections in the low shops in which they are now only sold, without thinking of the fat old bath-woman, who was a terror to me and others of my size and age. In 1816 these baths were discontinued and pulled down on the opening of George's Pier-head baths. For a mile or more there was good bathing on the shore. The bathing machines were introduced about the end of the last century. The keeper of the "Wishing Gate-house" had several, and an old man who lived in a low hut near the mill (the remains of which still stand in the Waterloo-road) had two or three, and made money by them. At that time Bootle and Bootle Marshes were wild places, the roads execrable, and as for frogs (Bootle organs), the noise they made at night was wonderful. I recollect all the docks and streets from Bath-street downwards being sand-hills and salt-marshes. New Quay, of which Bath-street was a continuation, was a sort of haven, into which small vessels, at certain times of the tide, ran to discharge their cargoes. On the tide receding the vessels were left high and dry upon the bank. Bathers used to be seen in any number on the shore. Decency was so frequently outraged that the authorities were at last compelled to take steps to redress the grievance. Not far from the baths was once a pleasant public walk of which I have often heard my father and mother speak. It was called the "Ladies Walk," and extended from the site of the present Canal bridge by Old Hall-street, down to the river. It was a sort of a terraced gravel walk, having four rows of fine Lombardy poplars, and seats underneath. On fine evenings all the gay and fashionable world of Liverpool used to take the air and show off their hoops and high heels, and the gentlemen their brocaded silk coats, and three-cornered hats. The sword was often drawn by the gallants for some fancied affront, and occasionally a little blood was spilt, a matter of no moment in those days. Great was the grief when it was announced that the Leeds and Liverpool Canal Company had resolved on the destruction of the Ladies Walk.

There was another Ladies Walk in Duke-street, which extended from opposite the present York-street (then called Great George-street) to Berry-street. This was afterwards converted into a ropery and succeeded by Parr-street. By the way, Duke-street, which occupies a portion of its site, has been famous for notable persons residing in it. In the third house from Colquitt-street Felicia Hemans was born, and she wrote some of her early poetry there. In the yard of the next house was once a tree, the last remnant of the Ladies Walk, which had two rows of trees down the sides and centre as in the other Ladies Walk previously mentioned. Mrs. Hemans apostrophizes this tree in one of her early poems. I recollect her very well, for she was intimate with my friends, the Nicholsons, who lived at the top of Richmond-row some forty years ago. Miss Browne received much advice and encouragement from Mr. Nicholson, and she was a most pleasing person. As Mrs. Hemans, her life was not happy. She resided at one time at Wavertree, in one of those cottages on the left hand side of the road just beyond Orford-street. The present "Loggerheads Tavern Revived" was Mr. Nicholson's house. It was a public-house, called "The Loggerheads" before he converted it into a private dwelling. Where Soho-street now begins there was a dyer's pond and yard; over it was a fine weeping-willow. In Duke-street also lodged at one time Thomas Campbell, the poet. He occupied part of the house now converted into a cabinet-maker's shop by Messrs. Abbot. I visited Mr. Campbell several times when he was preparing "The Pleasures of Hope" for publication. He was a very handsome young man, with a fine face and bright eyes. Mr. John Howard lodged in Duke-street in the house directly facing Cornwallis-street, then newly built. At this time his "Report on Prisons" was passing through the Warrington Press; and he used to journey backwards and forwards to correct the proofs. The Rev. Gilbert Wakefield lodged in Duke-street, near the bottom, when he was first appointed curate to St. Paul's church, then just erected. Dr. Henderson was the first incumbent of that church. Strangely enough, he seceded from the Dissenting body, while Mr. Wakefield joined it from the Church.

Curious stories were told of Dr. Henderson's ministration. Mr. Wakefield complained bitterly of the unkindness and inhospitality of the Liverpool clergy. He said he never was invited but by one brother clergyman to visit him during his stay in Liverpool.

In 1812, Bellingham, who shot Mr. Percival in the House of Commons, on the 11th of May, also lived in Duke-street, about the sixth house above Slater-street. His wife was a dressmaker and milliner. She was a very nice person, and after Bellingham's execution the ladies of Liverpool raised a subscription for, and greatly patronized her. Bellingham was born at St. Neot's, in Huntingdonshire, about 1771. His father was a land-surveyor and miniature-painter. Becoming insane, he was for some time confined in St. Luke's Hospital, London; but being found incurable he was taken home, where he died soon afterwards. Bellingham, at the age of fourteen, was apprenticed to a jeweller in Whitechapel, named Love, from whom, after giving much trouble and annoyance, he ran away. In 1786 his mother's sister's husband, a Mr. Daw, yielding to the solicitations of his wife and Mrs. Bellingham, fitted the young man out for India, whither he sailed in the ship *Hartwell*, in the Company's service. This vessel was wrecked off one of the Cape de Verd Islands, and young Bellingham managed to get home again, penniless—having lost everything he possessed. Still influenced by his female relatives, Mr. Daw next took a shop in the tinware trade for Bellingham. This shop was in Oxford-street; but a fire occurring in it, Bellingham asserted that he had a large number of bank-notes destroyed. It was suspected he was cognizant of the origin of this fire; but nothing could be proved against him. In 1794 he became bankrupt; but his creditors were so disgusted with the statement of his affairs, that they would not grant him his certificate, and he never obtained it. We next find him obtaining employment in a merchant's counting-house; and after being with them some time he was sent out by them to Archangel. He remained there about three years, and then entered into partnership with a firm there. He then came to Hull where he entered into contracts for the delivery of £12,000 worth of timber, but only £4,000 worth was ever delivered upon the bills drawn, accepted, and paid. Upon this transaction Bellingham was arrested and imprisoned in Hull, where he remained seven months. On his release he went back to Archangel, where he had no sooner arrived than he was again thrown into prison. He appealed vehemently against this arrest to the English Consul, and also to the British Ambassador at St. Petersburg, Lord Levison Gower; but they both declined interfering, as they considered his arrest legal and justifiable. On his release he came to Liverpool, whence he went to Dublin, where he met his future wife, Miss Neville, a native of Newry. Having become possessed of a legacy of £400, left him by his aunt, Mrs. Daw, he returned to Liverpool, where he commenced business as an Insurance and General Broker. He now began memorializing the government on the subject of his claims upon Russia. General Gascoigne presented his petitions. All he got was a constant refusal of interference. There is no doubt that some of the wrongs he complained of were partly imaginary, and that he perhaps inherited his father's malady. Finding his appeals of no avail he determined upon being revenged in some way or other upon somebody. On the 11th May, 1812, he posted himself, soon after five o'clock, near the door of the lobby of the House of Commons, and as Mr. Spencer Percival approached, he drew a pistol from his breast pocket, and fired at the right honourable gentleman. The shot took effect, and Mr. Percival died almost immediately afterwards. General Gascoigne, one of the members for Liverpool, was one of the first to recognize the assassin, and, in fact, seized him and took from him his pistols. It was not thought he had any particular enmity against Mr. Percival, but that he would have assassinated any other of His Majesty's Ministers had they fallen in his way at the time. He said he had been a fortnight making up his mind to this bloody deed. He bought his pistols from a well-known gunmaker in Fleet-street, and so desirous was he that they could be depended upon, that he went to Primrose Hill, in the outskirts of London, to try them. It was said that he had his coat altered, and a capacious and readily accessible pocket made in it; in which pocket, in fact, the discharged pistol was found. Bellingham to the last maintained his contumacious and determined character. He justified his frightful deed, and expressed himself resigned to his fate and prepared to meet it. His atrocious act caused a great sensation in the town. The news that it had been perpetrated, had, however, scarcely reached us in Liverpool before we heard of his trial and execution. He was tried on the 16th of May and executed on the 18th. Short shriving was then the mode!

In Suffolk-street, which runs out of Duke-street, there once dwelt a droll person named Peter Tyrer. He let out coaches and horses for hire. Many funny stories were current about him. I recollect one to the effect that a customer of his, a gentleman residing in Duke-street, complained several times that Peter had supplied him with a coach so stiff in the springs as to be quite unpleasant to ride in it. The next time a coach was sent for by this gentleman, Peter sent him a hearse! On being asked his reason for so doing, his reply was that "so many people had ridden in that vehicle and never made any complaint, that he supposed it must be a very comfortable conveyance."

# CHAPTER IV.

Before I exhaust my recollections of Duke-street and its celebrities, I ought not to omit mention of a worthy gentleman who resided in it, and whose name occupied the attention of the public in many ways, in all honourable to himself, as a man, a soldier, and a citizen. I refer to Colonel Bolton, whose mansion in Duke-street, between Suffolk-street and Kent-street (called after, and by Mr. Kent, who lived at the corner of the street, and who also named the streets adjacent after the southern counties), was in bye-gone years the head-quarters of the Tory party in Liverpool, in election times. From the balcony of that house, wherein the utmost hospitality was always exercised, the great statesmen who have represented Liverpool in Parliament—George Canning and William Huskisson—have many a time poured forth the floods of their eloquence, stirring up the heart's-blood of the thousands assembled in the street to hear them, making pulses beat quicker, and exciting passions to fever-heat. Mr. Canning used also to address the electors from Sir Thomas Brancker's house in Rodney-street.

The lengths to which election zeal carried men may be understood, when, during the progress of an election, business was suspended in the town for days and days. Hatred, envy, and malice were engendered. Neighbour was set against neighbour, and I have known many instances where serious divisions in families have taken place when opposite sides in politics have been chosen by the members of such families. It has required years to heal wounds made in family circles, and time in some instances never succeeded in bringing relatives to esteem each other again. The small knot of reformers in this town stuck manfully together and fought their battles well; and if the Tory side could boast of substantial names amongst their ranks, those of Henry Brougham, Egerton Smith, Dr. Shepherd, Mr. Mulock, Edward Rushton, and many others, occupy a place in the pantheon of worthies who stood forward on all great and public occasions when improvement in the constitution was to be advocated. I recollect a time when it was scarcely wise for a man to confess himself a reformer. At the beginning of this century, when the horrors of the French Revolution were fresh in all men's minds, and knowing so well as we did that there were many mischievous, dangerous, and disaffected people amongst us, ripe and ready to foment and foster broils, bringing anarchy and confusion in their train, it seemed to be the duty of all men who had characters and property to lose, to stick fast to the state as it was, without daring to change anything, however trifling or however necessary. A man was almost thought a traitor to talk of reform or change at one time, for there were not a few influential men who would rather have risen on the ruins of Old England than have fallen with her glory. Ticklish times we had in the beginning of the present century.

On the subject of Reform, it was said that an elector one day meeting Mr. Brougham in Castle-street, thus accosted him:—"Well, Mister, so you are going to try for Reform again?" "Yes," said the great orator, "and I hope we shall get it." Elector:—"Very good, Mister, we really do want a reform in parliament, for I think it is a very hard thing that a man can only get a paltry £5 or £10 for his vote. There ought to be some fixed sum—certainly not less than £25."

One of the most remarkable election events that has taken place in Liverpool was that in which Messrs. Ewart and Denison were engaged in 1830. Remarkable not only for the vigour with which it was carried on, but for the intense excitement that it created, the number of days it occupied, and also for the enormous sums of money it cost. The bribery that took place on both sides and all sides was really frightful. It was a positive disgrace to humanity. The contest was continued for seven days. While it was carried on business in the town was partly suspended, and all men's thoughts, and acts, and interests, seemed engrossed by the one prevailing subject. On the death of Mr. Huskisson, those interested in political matters set about to look for a successor to represent their interests in parliament. Several distinguished gentlemen were invited to stand; amongst others were Sir Robert Peel, and the Right Hon. Charles Grant, both of whom, however, declined the honour. Mr. Grant had had enough of an election contest to last him for some time, his success at Inverness had only been won by too hard fighting to be lightly thought of; while Sir Robert Peel freely confessed that the duties of Home Secretary were such as to prevent him from devoting sufficient time to the interests of so large and important a constituency as that of Liverpool.

By the way, I recollect a rather curious anecdote of Mr. Huskisson, which may perhaps not be devoid of interest. About 1834 I was dining on board one of the beautiful American sailing-packets, the *George Washington*. It was only a small party, and amongst others present was the late Sir George Drinkwater, who related the following curious circumstance connected with Mr. Huskisson:—Sir George told us that the day before the lamentable occurrence took place, which deprived this town of a valuable representative, and the country of so distinguished a statesman, Mr. Huskisson called upon him at the Town Hall (Sir George being then Mayor), and asked permission to write a letter. While doing so an announcement was made that there was a deputation from Hyde, near Manchester, wishing to see Mr. Huskisson. "Oh!" said that gentleman, "I know what they want; but I will send them back to Hyde with a flea in their ears!" The gentlemen of the deputation having been ushered into the room, they stated their case, to the effect that they solicited Mr. Huskisson to support a petition in parliament to enable them to construct a railway between their town and Manchester. They had no sooner stated their errand than Mr. Huskisson, angrily throwing down his pen, in very few words refused their request, winding up his reply with these memorable words—remarkable not only for the fallacy of his then opinions, but also in connection with the calamitous event of the next day— "Gentlemen, I supported the scheme of the railway between Liverpool and Manchester as an experiment, but as long as I have the honour to hold a seat in parliament, *I will never consent to see England gridironed by railways!*" What would Mr. Huskisson say now-a-days, when a map of England shows it not only gridironed, but spread over as with an iron net-work of railroads, that to the eye appear in a state of a inextricable entanglement?

To return to the election of 1830. During seven days the town was kept at fever-heat, each day its intensity becoming heightened. Denison, in his opening address on 'Change, on the 14th October, in appealing to the constituency for support, avowed himself entitled to it, not only as being Mr. Huskisson's friend—"the friend of your friend"—but an enthusiastic admirer of his principles. Mr. Denison was son-in-law to the Duke of Portland. Mr. Ewart was a townsman, and a barrister, and had represented the town of Bletchingly (or Bl*eeching*ly, as they call it in Surrey), so that both candidates came well recommended. The writ was moved for in the House of Commons on the 17th November, and received in Liverpool on the Friday following. An army of canvassers was organised on both sides, who plied their vocations in all directions. Mr. Denison's friends mustered on Tuesday morning, 23rd November, in front of Mr. Bolton's house in Duke-street, and moved in grand procession to the Town Hall. Amongst them were Mr. Bolton, Mr. Gladstone, Sir J. Tobin, Messrs. Wm. Brown, Ritson, Shand, and Garnett. Mr. Ewart's friends met opposite to the Adelphi Hotel. The horses were taken from Mr. Ewart's carriage, which was then drawn by the people. With Mr. Ewart were Messrs. J. Brancker, Hugh Jones, W. Wallace Currie, W. Earle, jun., Hall (barrister), Captain Colquitt, Rev. Wm. Shepherd, etc. The processions were both got up in admirable style; splendid and costly banners and flags of all descriptions were displayed, while ribbons, of which Denison's were scarlet, and Ewart's blue, fluttered in the wind in all directions. The following was the result of the polls. I give it to show how remarkably close the contest was carried on, and how the tide of favour ebbed and flowed: 1st day—Denison, 260; Ewart, 248. 2nd day—Denison, 583; Ewart, 568. 3rd day—Denison, 930; Ewart, 918. 4th day—Denison; 1320; Ewart, 1308. 5th day—Denison, 1700; Ewart, 1688. 6th day—Denison, 2020; Ewart, 2008. 7th day—Denison, 2186; Ewart, 2215. The number of freemen who voted was 4401.

If ever a borough deserved disfranchising, it was Liverpool on that election. The conduct of the freemen was atrocious. I speak of them as a body. The bribery on that occasion was so broad, barefaced, and unblushingly carried on, as to excite disgust in all thoughtful men's minds. Sums of money £3 to £100 were said to have been given for votes, and I recollect that after the heat of the election had subsided, a list of those who voted was published, with the sums attached, which were paid to and received by each freeman. I have a copy of it in my possession. Whether true or false who can tell? Where there is fire there will be smoke. It is a well-known fact that many of the canvassers never looked behind them after that memorable time, and numbers of tradesmen signally benefited by the money that was spread about with such liberal hands. In some cases money was received by freemen from both parties. In one case I find a man (among the H's) voting for Mr. Denison, who received £35 and £10. Amongst the C's was a recipient of £28 and £25 from each side; and another, a Mr. C., took £50 from Denison and £15 from Ewart, the said voter being a chimney-sweeper, and favouring Mr. Denison with the weight of his influence and the honour of his suffrage. In looking over the list I find that the principal recipients of the good things going, were ropers, coopers, sailmakers, and shipwrights. Yet the name of "merchant" and "tradesman" not unfrequently occurs in the descriptions of borough voters. Amongst the W's there appears to be scarcely a voter that escaped "the gold fever." Amongst others who declined taking any part in the election was Mr. Brooks Yates; he, feeling so disgusted with the veniality of the voters, and the bribery that was going on, publicly protested on the seventh day against the conduct of all parties, and said "he lifted up his voice against the practice of bribery, which was so glaringly exercised, and which had been carried on by both parties to the utmost extent. The friends of Mr. Ewart had made use of his name to fill up their complement without his authority, and he begged to withdraw it, for he was resolved to remain decidedly neutral. The corruption was so gross and flagrant that he would not give his vote on either side." It is said that this election cost upwards of £100,000, of which sum Colonel Bolton supplied £10,000. Mr. Ewart's family it was understood, entirely furnished his expenses amounting to £65,000. Mr. Denison's reached from £47,000 to £50,000.

Amongst those who addressed the various meetings during the week of the election, and previous to the commencement of the polling, were Mr. William Rathbone, Mr. Henderson, barrister (afterwards recorder), Rev. W. Shepherd, Captain Colquitt, Mr. James Brancker (who proposed and seconded Mr. Ewart), and Mr. Falvey. The orators on the part of Mr. Denison were, Mr. Edward Rushton (afterwards stipendiary magistrate), Messrs. Shand, W. Brown (now Sir William Brown), John Bolton, W. Earle, Leyland, Sir John Tobin, etc. About the fourth day of the election the real excitement commenced, and the baneful system of bribery was resorted to. On the fifth day the prices of votes advanced from £20 to £25, and as much as £40 to £50 were asked and obtained. It was expected that on the sixth day the contest would close, but it seemed to be then continued with unabated vigour. On the seventh day voters were brought from all parts of England, Scotland, Ireland, and wherever they could be met with. The tricks played by both parties on voters were most amusing, either to deter or compel them to vote. Nearly four hundred freemen declined or were unable to record their votes.

Even in the elections for mayor the most inconceivable interest was excited, and in one case, that of 1828, between Messrs. Porter and Robinson, from £16,000 to £20,000, if not a larger sum, was said to have been expended in carrying the day. I recollect a worthy tobacconist, who kept a little shop in the town, who had a vote and was not inclined to sell it cheap. In every insidious way was he assailed to part with his vote. On the occasion of this election the list of voters was rapidly running out to the last drop; the hour of closing the poll was approaching, and it was found impossible to keep the poll open another day. "Come, Mr. Pipes, what about your vote?—it's half-past three!" "Call again in a quarter of an hour." In this quarter of an hour the little tobacconist's shop was besieged by canvassers on both sides, when the tempting sum of £30 was reached. The cunning little Abel Drugger knew his value, but no higher sum would either party advance. Pipes had, unfortunately, gone into the back part of his shop for a few minutes, when a wag put his clock back thirteen minutes. Keeping his eye, while in the shop, on the clock, every now and then—although, as he admitted afterwards, it seemed a long quarter of an hour—he still kept off his persecutors. When the hand approached the quarter on the false-telling dial, one canvasser, bolder than the rest, laid £35 on a box of cigars, as the bid for it. But Master Pipes only was sold, for just as he was about to take up the tissue paper bearing the magic name of Henry Hase, St. George's church struck four, and the prize was re-pocketed to the great discomfiture of "Pipes," and the merriment of his customers. Of electioneering tricks I could tell a full score.

The practice of the "Duello" is, happily, now gone quite out of fashion, but in my young days any and every occasion of offence was seized upon as a *casus belli*. Duels were fought on the most frivolous occasions and for the slightest possible affronts, intentional or supposititious.

This taste has subsided, as well as that for hard drinking. I can remember both being carried to a lamentable state of excess; but these practices have grown out of date. I have seen, thank goodness, other equally salutary improvements in morals, customs, and manners.

Two remarkable hostile meetings, I recollect, took place in Liverpool at the commencement of the present century, and caused an immense sensation, from the known position and high standing of all the parties concerned.

The first duel I shall mention was that between Mr. Sparling, late of St. Domingo House, Everton, and Mr. Grayson, an eminent shipbuilder. Both gentlemen moved in the first circles of society in the town. It took place on the 24th of February, 1804.

The occasion of the duel was a conversation that occurred in Mr. Grayson's carriage, between that gentleman and Major Brooks (who was shot by Colonel Bolton in the ensuing year), on their way to dine at Mr. Grayson's, at Wavertree. Mr. Grayson, it seems, called Mr. Sparling "a villain," for breaking off the marriage between himself and a relative of Mr. Grayson's. Major Brooks repeated this conversation to Mr. Sparling, who instantly commenced a correspondence with Mr. Grayson, calling upon him to apologise for his language. This correspondence continued from October until the time the duel was fought—the meeting being the consequence of the unsatisfactory results of the communications between the parties. They met at a place called Knot's Hole, near the shore by the Aigburth-road. Mr. Sparling was attended by Captain Colquitt, commanding the *Princess* frigate, then in the river. Mr. Grayson's second was Dr. MacCartney. After the fatal shots were fired Mr. Grayson's servant found his master alone, lying on the ground with his face downwards. He was desperately wounded in the thigh, and was taken back to Liverpool as quickly as possible. He lingered until the following Sunday, when he died. Mr. Sparling and Captain Colquitt were, at the coroner's inquest, found guilty of murder, and were tried at Lancaster, on the 4th of April, before Sir Alan Chambre. Sergeant Cockle, Attorney-General for the County Palatine of Lancaster, led for the crown; with him were Messrs. Clark and Scarlett (afterwards Sir James); attorneys, Messrs. Ellames and Norris. For the prisoners, Messrs. Park (afterwards Baron Park), Wood, Topping, Raincock, and Heald; attorney, Mr. William Statham.

It came out in evidence during the trial, that the hour of meeting was seven o'clock on Sunday morning, February 24th. Mr. Sparling and Captain Colquitt arrived first at Park Chapel; on alighting the Captain carried the pistol-case, and the two gentlemen went through a gate into a field opposite, to the place of rendezvous. Soon after Dr. MacCartney and Mr. Park, the surgeon, arrived in a carriage. Mr. Park had been induced to accompany the Doctor on the representation that he was about to attend a patient of some consequence, and required his (Mr. Park's) advice and skill. Soon after Mr. Grayson arrived on foot, attended by his servant, when, finding the two gentlemen in waiting, he pulled out his watch, and remarked that he feared he was rather late, but that it was all his servant's fault. Dr. MacCartney then took out the pistol-case from the carriage (leaving Mr. Park in it, who had declined proceeding any further), and with Mr. Grayson passed through the same gate as did Mr. Sparling and the Captain. They then went down the field towards the river, and soon afterwards a shot or shots were heard by Mr. Park, Mr. Grayson's servant, and the post-boys. Mr. Grayson's servant ran into the field, and met Mr. Sparling and Captain Colquitt hurrying up the foot-road, the former asked him "what he wanted?" he told him who he was, when Mr. Sparling informed him his master was severely wounded. The two gentlemen then ran onward when they met Mr. Park, who had got out of the carriage on seeing them coming towards the road in such a hurry. They bade him "make haste, for Grayson was badly wounded." They then got into their carriage and told the coachman to drive back to Liverpool. The other driver asserted he heard Captain Colquitt say, "by G---, it has done me good." The two gentlemen were driven first to Mr. Ralph Benson's in Duke-street, to whom a message was sent up that Mr. Sparling "had been in the country and was quite well." They next called on Mr. Stavert, when Mr. Sparling said, "I have put a ball into Grayson this morning." Mr. Stavert replied, "I hope he is not much hurt," when Mr. Sparling exclaimed, "I think not, for he made too much noise for it to be of any consequence." They were next driven to the Royal Hotel and thence to the Pier Slip, where a boat was in waiting, in which they were rowed off.

Mr. Park, on hurrying forward to Knot's Hole, found Mr. Grayson supported by his servant and Dr. MacCartney. His breeches were soaked with blood at his right thigh. There appeared to be a shot-hole at the upper part near the hip. He complained of being in acute pain, and that he had lost the use of his limbs; he said he could no longer stand, but must be allowed to sit down. The party, however, bore him to the carriage, and got him home as soon as possible. Mr. Park attended him until he died. The ball had perforated the thigh-bone, and was not extracted until after death. It was produced in court.

Mr. Grayson was fully aware of his approaching end. On the Wednesday after the duel, he told Mr. Park that "he was going to meet his God." On the following day he said that "he hoped for mercy, and that he might have gone with greater guilt on his head, if he had killed Sparling, instead of Sparling killing him"; and added, "whatever his opinions of Mr. Sparling's conduct might be, he truly forgave him the injury he had done him, in giving him his death-wound, and hoped, in the event of his decease, that his friends would not prosecute him." Mr. Grayson repeatedly said Mr. Sparling was an utter stranger to him, and that he did not know him even by sight.

At that time counsel were not allowed to make any appeal to a jury for a prisoner. Mr. Sparling's defence was therefore read by one of his counsel, Mr. Park. It was very ably got up. He bitterly protested against the outcry that had been made against him in public, from the pulpit and by the press. He wholly denied bearing any malice towards Mr. Grayson, and justified himself, declaring his act was a mere vindication of his honour and good name, and that he had, in conjunction with Captain Colquitt, repeatedly asked Mr. Grayson to withdraw his insulting words and threatening speeches, but without avail, and the meeting was the consequence of his obstinacy. He said of Mr. Grayson, as Mr. Grayson had said of him, that he was an utter stranger to him. Captain Colquitt made an able defence, wherein he justified himself and his conduct. A number of gentlemen of high character and distinction spoke to the kindliness of manner of Mr. Sparling at all times, and also of Captain Colquitt, and completely exonerated them from the imputation of entertaining vindictive or malevolent feelings. Amongst others who appeared for Mr. Sparling were Sir Hungerford Hoskins, Captain Palmer, Rev. Jonathan Brooks, His Worship the Mayor (William Harper, Esq.), Soloman D'Aguilar, Lord Viscount Carleton, Major-General Cartwright, Lord Robert Manners, Lord Charles Manners, Lord James Murray, Colonel M'Donald, and Major Seymour. For Captain Colquitt many equally honourable gentlemen and officers in His Majesty's service gave evidence in his favour.

The judge on summing up decidedly leaned towards the prisoners, and the result was a verdict of "Not Guilty." The same jury was afterwards empanelled to try Mr. Sparling, Captain Colquitt, and Dr. MacCartney on another indictment, but no evidence being brought forward, they were all acquitted.

Thus terminated a trial which created an immense amount of interest, not only in Liverpool, but throughout the whole of the northern counties.

Before I relate the incidents of the second duel that took place in Liverpool, I will briefly give the particulars of another affair, which happened in the same year (July, 1804), which gave the gossips and *quid nuncs* of the town ample food for conversation. This was the court-martial on Captain Carmichael, the Adjutant of Colonel Earle's regiment of Fusiliers, and formerly adjutant of Colonel Bolton's regiment of "Royal Liverpool Volunteers." He was charged with "disobedience of orders, and with addressing Colonel Earle in abusive and scandalous language respecting the officers of the regiment." The court-martial was held by virtue of a warrant from His Royal Highness Prince William Frederick of Gloucester, the General commanding the district. The president was Colonel Bolton; the judge-advocate, Fletcher Raincock, Esq., barrister-at-law.

It appeared that on the 12th of June the Fusiliers were drilling on Copperas-hill (fancy *our* Volunteers drilling on Copperas-hill!), at the manual and platoon exercise, when they were commanded to "order arms" and "stand at ease" by the Colonel; his intention being to keep the regiment for the remainder of the morning at firelock exercise. Something was said of a private nature by Colonel Earle to the Adjutant Carmichael, who, instead of replying, took no notice of the observation. He subsequently spoke to the Colonel in an insulting and impertinent manner, treating him at the same time with marked indignity—calling out, loud enough for the men to hear, "that he insisted upon the officers being called together to inquire into his conduct, for such things were said of him as he could not bear." On being told that that was not the time nor place to bring charges against the officers, and that he should put down in writing what he had to say, and he would then be attended to, he did not seem satisfied, but continued to demand the calling of the officers together. Colonel Earle told him to go on with his duty. Captain Carmichael still took no notice of these orders; but said his feelings were "worked up to a fiddle-string." Still disobeying Colonel Earle's commands, he was told "to go home if he could not do his duty." He was then heard to say that the officers, or some of the officers, were "a set of blacklegs." For this offence Captain Carmichael was tried. He denied at first the right of the court to sit in judgment upon him, and raised three objections, two of which were read, and the third was stopped in the middle, being overruled by the court. The court-martial sat five days, and the result of it was that Captain Carmichael was acquitted of disobedience, but found guilty of addressing abusive language to his commanding-officer. His sentence was "to be reprimanded at the head of his regiment." Colonel Bolton was delegated to administer this reproof. Colonel Bolton spoke highly in the Captain's favour, and stated that he had presented him with a piece of plate which he had bought for him when in London, to mark his respect for him, and his efficiency in drilling his (Colonel Bolton's) regiment.

In the following year, 1805, the second duel was fought, which created as great a sensation as that between Mr. Sparling and Mr. Grayson, in the previous year. In this encounter the principals were Colonel Bolton and Major Brooks, the same party who had caused the mischief in the previously-mentioned affair.

The origin of the quarrel arose in this way:—Colonel Bolton, who had raised a regiment of volunteers, in 1803, which he had entirely clothed, armed, and equipped, mustering ten companies of sixty men each, was held in high respect and possessed great influence with government. On the death of Mr. Bryan Blundell, who held the appointment of Customs Jerker, Colonel Bolton obtained the vacant office for Major Brooks, who had been formerly in the Lancashire Militia. After enjoying this place for a time, Major Brooks applied for an increase of salary. His application was referred to the West India Association, of which Colonel Bolton was President, to report upon whether an increase in the pay of the office was desirable or deserved. The Association reported adverse to Major Brooks' application. He immediately, publicly, and in the most disgraceful manner, accused Colonel Bolton with being the cause of this refusal, as he had learnt that the Colonel had said that "£700 a year was quite income enough for a comparatively young, unmarried man." Major Brooks, forgetting that Colonel Bolton's friendship and influence had obtained for him, in the first instance, his appointment, did his utmost to force his benefactor into collision with him, and to such an extent was this annoyance carried, that at length a hostile meeting was arranged between the parties. As a soldier and gentleman, Colonel Bolton could no longer keep quiet. Major Brooks possessed, unfortunately for himself, a great amount of irritable vanity and pugnacity. He had been "out," as it was then called, not long before with Captain Carmichael, whose trial by court-martial I have just detailed, upon some point of difference in military discipline. The meeting took place on Bootle Sands, and, to show Major Brooks's temper, on Captain Carmichael firing in the air, he exclaimed: "D--- it, why don't you fire at me—we did not come here for child's play!" In those days duelling was very prevalent, and small words brought out pistols and coffins for two.

The first meeting between Colonel Bolton and Major Brooks was to have come off on the 20th December, 1804, at a place called Miller's Dam, off the Aigburth-road, which, if I recollect rightly, was a small creek which ran up to a mill—long and long ago swept away. The circumstance of the quarrel, however, having by some means got abroad, the authorities interposed and both gentlemen were arrested on their way to the rendezvous. They were both bound over, in very heavy penalties, to keep the peace to all and sundry of His Majesty's subjects, and each other in particular, for twelve calendar months. Brooks, on being arrested, exhibited the utmost rage and virulence, and expressed himself in strong language against the Colonel, accusing him roundly of being the cause of the arrest, and the interference they had met with. There was not word of truth in this charge, Colonel Bolton, though forced into the matter, according to the laws of honour, kept the meeting a secret, and it was afterwards actually proved that the secret of the meeting oozed out from one of Major Brooks' own friends.

During the twelve months the two gentlemen were bound over, Brooks let slip no opportunity of insulting Colonel Bolton, as far as he dared without coming into actual collision. He said he was the cause of their meeting being interrupted, although he had been frequently assured of the truth. As the twelve months were about to expire, Major Brooks increased his violence. On the day the bond ceased to have effect, the Major, meeting Colonel Bolton walking with Colonel Earle past the shop, kept at present by Mr. Allender, in Castle-street, then and there publicly again insulted him, and called him by a name which no gentleman could put up with. A challenge was the consequence. The report of the disturbance soon reached the Exchange, and the authorities again stepped forward to prevent hostilities. Colonel Bolton was again arrested and bound over, and Major Brooks was taken into custody. The latter denied the right of the authorities to arrest him, asserting that he had done nothing of sufficient weight to break his bond, and that he could not be again bound over until the year of bondage had expired. The Major was some hours in custody, but was at length released without promising anything. He was no sooner at liberty than he sent a friend to Colonel Bolton, who consented to a meeting for that very afternoon. This was on the 20th of December, 1805. The place of rendezvous on this occasion was in a field at the foot of Love-lane (now called Fairclough-lane), which was skirted by it. The exact spot of meeting was in a field about half-way between the present Boundary-street (then a narrow lane with hedges) and St. Jude's Church. It was near Fielding's nursery ground, which occupied the land now used as a timber-yard. It was quite dark when the combatants arrived. Major Brooks was accompanied Mr. Forbes. Mr. Park, surgeon, who resided at the corner of Newington-bridge, was taken up by Colonel Bolton on his way to the place of meeting in his carriage. Mr. Harris was Colonel Bolton's second. When the parties got over into the field it was found that they could not see to load the pistols. It would then be about six o'clock. Candles were therefore procured to enable them to complete the necessary arrangements.

As soon as the combatants had taken the places allotted to them, Colonel Bolton observed that, according to the laws of honour and duelling, the Major was entitled to fire first. To this the Major assented, and fired immediately, the shot passing harmlessly by the Colonel, who then fired in his turn, hitting Major Brooks in the right eye. The Major instantly fell and died. Colonel Bolton was hurried off and remained in concealment for a short time. It was said that the firing of the pistols was heard in Major Brooks' house at the corner of Daulby-street. An inquiry was held, when a verdict of wilful murder was found, but in consequence of the strong recommendations of Major Brooks's friends, admitting that he was entirely to blame, and that his dreadful fate was entirely brought on by himself, the matter passed over without further notice, everyone admitting that Colonel Bolton had conducted himself with the utmost forbearance as well as courage, and that he deserved the highest encomiums for his gentlemanly and straightforward behaviour throughout this most painful affair.

# CHAPTER V.

Some five years previous to this event, about the month of June, 1800, a circumstance occurred which created a great sensation in the town, and occupied public attention in a most remarkable degree. It seems rather out of chronological order to go back five years; but the reader who favours me with his attention must be content to obtain my information as I can impart it. My head is not so clear as it used to be in the arrangement of such matters.

In the year mentioned there was a merchant established in Liverpool of the name of Wainwright, who was one of the actors in what nearly proved to be a tragedy. At a place called Tunstall, near Burslem, in Staffordshire, resided an earthenware manufacturer named Theophilus Smith. This Smith was in difficulties and his affairs were in much disorder. His creditors were hostile to him, and he for some time had been endeavouring to obtain a settlement with them. Amongst other creditors was Mr. Wainwright. He, however, was not one of the hostile party, but was very well-disposed towards Mr. Smith. One day, in the month of June, Mr. Wainwright received an anonymous letter, requesting him to meet the writer at a small public-house near the "Olympic Circus," which was a temporary place of amusement erected in Christian-street, then beginning to be built upon (the Adelphi Theatre in Christian-street succeeded the Circus—in fact, this place of amusement was called "the Circus" for many years). Mr. Wainwright, on carefully examining the letter, fancied he recognised Smith's handwriting, and resolved upon keeping the appointment, supposing that Smith, fearing arrest, dared not openly wait upon him. An arrest was an easy matter then. It was only necessary to swear to a debt and take out a writ and you could arrest anybody at a moment's notice, whether they actually owed you anything or not. There used to be tough swearing in olden times. Mr. Wainwright went to the house indicated and there, as he anticipated, found Theophilus Smith. Mr. Wainwright concluded that Smith was about to make some disclosures relative to his affairs and that was the reason he had sent for him. But Smith only produced a printed statement of his accounts, which had been previously circulated, and made no new discovery of any consequence; he, however, most strongly and earnestly entreated Mr. Wainwright to accompany him to Tunstall, where, he said, on the following afternoon, his creditors would meet, and where Mr. Wainwright's presence would be conducive to their coming to terms. Mr. Wainwright at first refused to accede to this request, having important business of his own to attend to, but Smith was so importunate that he at length consented to accompany him, and they set out on the same afternoon in a chaise and pair. On their way, Smith was very friendly with Mr. Wainwright, and conversed with him as any man would with a friendly traveller on a long journey. On arriving within a mile of his house at Tunstall, Mr. Smith ordered the chaise to be stopped, and got out, and requested Mr. Wainwright to do the same, saying that a mile could be saved by walking across some fields adjacent. Mr. Smith at the time expressed his dread of being arrested if he were seen on the road along which the chaise would have to be driven. Mr. Wainwright, however, declined to get out; stating it was quite unnecessary to take so much precaution; but at length, in consequence of Smith's earnest entreaty, he consented. They then proceeded across the fields on foot. As it was commencing to rain, Mr. Smith pressed on Mr. Wainwright the use of his cloak; but this Mr. Wainwright declined. Smith then led the way across the fields, by a stile path, till they arrived at length at a small thicket, through which they proceeded, when Smith stopped short, and said he knew a nearer way. Smith then led Mr. Wainwright into a meadow, and standing before him drew out a pistol. Mr. Wainwright immediately concluded that his fellow-passenger intended to put an end to his own life, and, after a sharp struggle, got the pistol from him, remonstrating with him upon the wickedness of the act. Smith, however, drew another pistol, and fired it at Mr. Wainwright, fortunately without effect. The latter instantly sprang upon Mr. Smith and got him down, uttering loud cries for assistance. Smith begged hard for mercy, and on promising not to repeat his murderous attack, was allowed to get up. He was no sooner released and on his legs than he drew a third pistol, fired, and hit Mr. Wainwright in the body. The men again closed, when Smith drew a knife and made several attempts upon his companion's life by attempting to cut his throat, which was fortunately well protected by the thick rolls of cambric it was then the custom to tie round the neck, as well as by a thick scarf, which was cut through in several places. Mr. Wainwright, however, never left hold of Smith until they reached his house when, the door suddenly opening, he rushed in and quickly closed it. He then came to the window and ordered Mr. Wainwright away, refusing him shelter, although it was growing dark and raining heavily. Mr. Wainwright contrived to crawl to a cottage, where he was laid up for some time, but eventually recovered from the cuts and wounds inflicted upon him. Smith absconded, and a reward of £50 was offered for his capture. This was effected after some time in Pall Mall, London, by two Bow-street runners. Smith was committed for trial at Stafford assizes, where he was found guilty and sentenced to be hung. He, however, escaped that punishment by destroying both himself and his wife in his cell in Stafford gaol, while awaiting his sentence. What Smith's motive could be for his conduct no one could conjecture. He would give no explanation on the subject though pressed to do so. It was supposed that a sudden fit of insanity had seized him, and that his violence was the result of it. During the journey the two gentlemen were on the most friendly terms, taking their meals together and acting as travellers thrown together usually do. Mr. Wainwright's presence was most essential to Smith to allay the hostility of his creditors, and therefore, the attempts to make away with him were still more incomprehensible.

As I sit by my fire-side with two or three old friends—friends, indeed, for I have known them all for fifty, sixty, and seventy years—we talk over old times, faces, scenes and places, in a way that calls up the ghosts of the past to our dim eyes. If my readers could listen to our stories of the old town they would hear more about it in a night than my little amanuensis could write down in a day. Many curious anecdotes and circumstances are called to remembrance by us, and I must say we talk of old times with a regretful yet pleasant feeling. I know I often startle some of my young friends by telling them of scenes I have witnessed in the last century, and I have often noticed them in their minds putting one year and another together, or subtracting one from another so that they might ascertain whether I was telling the truth or not.

I don't believe there is another man in Liverpool alive at this time who saw the Town Hall on fire in 1795. I saw it, I may say, almost break out, for I was in Castle-street in ten minutes after the alarm had spread through the town, and that was soon done, for Liverpool was not of the extent it is now. I believe half the inhabitants turned out into the streets to witness that awful sight, although it was at five o'clock on a frosty Sunday morning in January. For my part, I was aroused by the continuous springing of rattles by the watchmen, and the rushing sounds of people running along the street. I was soon out of bed and joined the throng of people who were hurrying to the scene of disaster. When I arrived there, a crowd had already assembled. Castle-street was then very narrow. It was quite choked up with people. Dale-street was beginning to be crowded while High-street and Water-street were quite impassable. From the windows of all the houses the terrified inmates were to be observed *en dishabille*, and the large inn in Water-street, the Talbot, which was nearly opposite the Town Hall, had people looking out at every window.

The smoke first made its appearance at the lower windows of the Town Hall. The doors having been forced, a party of men got into the interior of the building, and brought out for safety the books of the various departments, and some of the town's officers having arrived, something like system took the place of the dreadful confusion which prevailed. The town records, the treasurer's accounts, and the muniments, etc., were safely removed to a house at the end of High-street. I helped to keep order. Assisted by many other volunteers for the work we formed a lane so that there should be no impediment to a quick removal of anything that was portable. The fire was first discovered about five o'clock in the morning by the watchman on duty in the street. They were dull old fellows, those watchmen, and of but little use, for in calling the hour nine times out of ten they made a mistake. The thieves laughed them to scorn. When the watchman saw smoke issuing from the windows he gave the alarm without delay. The fire soon showed itself, when it had once got ahead. When the new Exchange was erected, after the former one had been taken down in 1748, somebody persuaded the authorities to have the woodwork and timber of the new building steeped in a composition of rosin and turpentine, so as to make the wood more durable. It may therefore be readily imagined how inflammable such a composition would make the wood, and how fiercely it burned when once ignited. There had been a perceptible odour of some sort experienced in the Exchange building for some days, and this was afterwards discovered to have arisen from the woodwork under the council-chamber having taken fire through a flue communicating from the Loan-office; and there is no doubt it had been smouldering for days before it actually made its appearance. It could not have been ten minutes after I arrived on the spot before the flames burst out in all their fury. It was an awfully grand sight. It was yet dark. What with the rushing and pushing of the anxious crowd, the roaring of the fierce flames, and the calling of distracted people, it was an event and scene never to be forgotten. The building was soon all in a blaze, and nothing on earth could have stopped that frightful conflagration. It was a mercy it was a calm frosty morning or the houses in the four streets adjacent must have caught the flame. From the age of these houses, the quantity of timber in them, the narrowness of the streets, and the absence of a copious supply of water, I am sure Liverpool would have been half consumed if a wind had sprung up. I thought the building looked like a great funeral pile as the flames roared out on all sides. It was a grand, yet dreadful sight. The whole of Castle-street was occupied by people, although, from the position of the Exchange, a full front view could not be obtained, it being almost parallel with the west side of Castle-street. The best view of it was where I stood at the top of Dale-street, by Moss's bank. The dome, being constructed of wood, soon took fire, was burnt, and fell in. We had not then as now powerful engines, long reels of hose, and bands of active men well trained to their arduous and dangerous duties, still, everybody did his best and seemed desirous of doing something. We did that something with a will, but without much order, system, or discretion. The engines in use were not powerful, and the supply of water was not only tardy but scanty, as you may believe when I tell you it had to be brought from the town wells, the Dye-house Well in Greetham-street, the Old Fall Well in Rose-street (where Alderman's Bennett's ironwork warehouse stands, near the corner of Rose-street—by the way, Rose-street was called after Mr. Rose, who lived in the house next the Stork Hotel), and the wells on Shaw's-brow; indeed, every possible source where water could be obtained, was put in requisition. The inhabitants allowed the rain-water to be taken from their water-butts in the vicinity to such liberal extent that I verily believe there was not a drop of rain-water to be got for love or money when that eventful day was out. Staid housewives for many a day after complained of the dirt the trampling of feet had made in their lobbies and yards, and deplored the loss of their stores of soft-water. At that time water was precious, every drop that could be obtained was saved, garnered, and carefully kept. Every drop of hard-water we consumed had to be brought to our doors and paid for by the "Hessian" or bucket. The water-carts were old butts upon wheels, drawn by sorry horses and driven by fat old creatures, half men half women in their attire and manners. The buckets were made of leather and the water was sold at a halfpenny per Hessian. They were so called, I believe, from their fancied resemblance to the Hessian boots. You may judge how inadequate a supply of water we had when our wants were dependent upon such aid. The water-carts came rumbling and tumbling along the streets, in many cases losing one-half of their loads by the unusual speed at which they were driven and the awkwardness of their drivers. Water was also carted from the river, and I helped with others to push the carts up Water-street. The steep ascent of this street in its badly paved condition made this work extremely laborious. But everybody helped and did what they could, and those who did nothing made up for deeds by words and shouted and bawled and told the others what they ought to do.

Fortunately, only one life was lost, that of a fool-hardy young man who would press forward to see the fire better—he rushed up to the High-street door and a piece of timber fell on him. The surging of the crowd caused several persons to be struck down and trampled upon. I saved one woman's life by beating off the people who would have crushed her. By twelve o'clock the fire had slackened considerably, and by the evening it was to all appearance subdued. But the fire in the interior remained smouldering for some time afterwards. In the churches on that day the event was alluded to in a very feeling manner, and in St. Peter's Church the rector offered up a prayer of thanksgiving that the town had been spared from a more extensive calamity.

At this time High-street (there was a famous tavern called the "Punch-Bowl" in this street) was the communication between Castle-street and Old Hall-street, and it is a most strange circumstance that the direct line of road was not retained instead of cutting the new street called Exchange-street East through the houses and gardens between Tithebarn-street and Dale-street. It was a great mistake, and everybody said so at the time. Many great mistakes have been made in respect to our streets and public buildings, not the least of which was the blunder of filling up the Old Dock, and erecting that huge and ugly edifice, the Custom-house, thereon.

I believe if the conflagration had extended from the Exchange to some distance in the adjoining streets, we should have had some vast improvements effected. From the narrowness of Castle-street may be imagined what a scene of confusion it must have been during the fire. It is quite a wonder that many lives were not lost during that morning of terror. The inhabitants of the four streets in many cases prepared for flight, for the fire raged so fiercely at one time that the escape of the houses in the vicinity from destruction seemed miraculous. While I was helping to draw water from the yard of some people I knew in Castle-street, a burning ember or piece of timber fell into a lot of dirty paper which would in five minutes have been alight if I had not been there to extinguish it. There were many such wonderful escapes recorded.

The trial of Mr. Charles Angus for the alleged murder of Miss Margaret Burns (who was his late wife's half-sister) in 1808, may be considered as one of the *causes celebres* of the time. It took place at Lancaster, on the 2nd of September, before Sir Alan Chambre. Sergeant Cockle, and Messrs. Holroyd, Raine and Clark, were for the Crown; Mr. T. Statham, attorney. Messrs. Topping, Scarlett, and Cross for the prisoner; Mr. Atkinson, attorney. Mr. Angus was a gentleman of Scotch birth, and resided in Liverpool—in King-street, I think. He had been at one time an assistant to a druggist, where he was supposed to have obtained a knowledge of the properties of poisons, and he was charged with putting this knowledge to account in attempting to produce abortion in the case of Miss Burns, who was suspected of being pregnant by him, and thereby causing her death. Miss Burns was Mr. Angus's housekeeper, and governess to his three children. The case rested entirely on circumstantial evidence, made out against the prisoner by his conduct previous to the supposed commission of the deed, by his conduct at the time and afterwards. At the time the strongest prejudice ran against Mr. Angus, and it must be said that the public were not satisfied with the verdict of the jury; but at this distance of time, those who had an opportunity of looking over the evidence, and remembering the case in all its bearings, will at once say dispassionately that there was not a shadow of evidence against

Mr. Angus. Miss Burns, who had been unwell for some time, was noticed previous to the 23rd of March, 1808, to be ailing, and that her size had materially enlarged; and it was suspected, as adduced by several witnesses, that she was *enceinte*. On the 23rd of March she complained of being very unwell, and went to lie down on a sofa in the breakfast-room where she remained the whole of the day, thirsting and vomiting. Mr. Angus would not allow his servants to sit up with Miss Burns, but remained in the room with her the whole of that night, the next day, and the following night. On the 25th Miss Burns said she felt better. A servant on that morning was sent to Henry-street for some Madeira that Miss Burns fancied. On her return, not seeing the lady on the sofa, where an hour previous she had left her, she looked round the room and discovered her doubled up in a corner of the room with her face towards the wainscot, while Mr. Angus was asleep sitting in a chair covered by a counterpane. The evidence was most conflicting. Several witnesses declared Miss Burns was not pregnant, others that they believed she was. The medical evidence was also of a most bewildering and diverse nature. Some of the most eminent surgeons in Liverpool were examined, and none of them agreed on the case. This fact came out that no signs of childbirth were visible as having taken place—no dead infant was discovered. The room in which Miss Burns and Mr. Angus were, was at all times accessible to the servants, and no cries of parturition were heard during the lady's illness. The fact of the matter was, Miss Burns had suffered from an internal complaint, and died from natural causes. This was shown by Dr. Carson, then a young and rising physician at the time, and who afterwards published a pamphlet in which he utterly demolished the medical evidence given at the trial for the crown.

The jury, after a few minutes' deliberation, returned a verdict, finding the prisoner "Not Guilty," on grounds as unimpeachable as the trial. In some of the circumstances attending and resulting from it, it was disgraceful, especially on the part of the medical witnesses for the crown, in their conduct towards the one for the defence—Dr. Carson. I have before me an authentic "Report of the Trial," "A Vindication of their Opinions," published by those witnesses, and Dr. Carson's "Remarks" on that publication, in which he exposes their shortcomings with a master's hand, in a style as terse as it is bold, and as elegant as it is severe; never were the weapons of irony, satire, and invective more effectively used; his impeachment is as withering as his victory at the trial was complete. The authors of the "Vindications" had not only done what in them lay to ruin him in every conceivable way, public and private, but they had exposed themselves to his "Remarks," all-pungent as they were, by going into court and giving opinions founded upon "the most disgracefully deficient dissection ever made." The sore which they had inflicted upon themselves at the trial did not heal under the caustic of the "Remarks"; and so the doctor became a victim to local prejudice, passion, and persecution. But he gained to himself a world-wide reputation which outlived them all; the honours of the French Academy were bestowed upon him, and he took his stand among the literary and scientific magnates of the day. As to the trial, the theory of the prosecution was that the prisoner caused the lady's death by administering a poison to procure abortion, and it was based upon a hole in the coats of the stomach, and a peculiar mark in the uterus; the medical witnesses for the crown affirming that the former could not have arisen from any other known cause than poison, and the latter a sure sign of recent delivery. No poison was found in the stomach or intestines, nor were the supposed contents of the uterus ever found, and no other part of the body was examined. The hole in the stomach presented the same appearance, and was described in the same terms as those which John Hunter had called attention to as occurring in certain cases of sudden death, where there was no suspicion of poisoning, and caused by the action of the gastric juice. Doctor Carson accepted Hunter's facts, but propounded a theory of his own, being guided to his conclusions by the experiments of Sir John Pringle and Dr. Bride, in reference to water at the temperature of 90 degrees dissolving animal substances. He successfully combated the notion about poisoning from another point of view, namely, the symptoms during life, the comparative mildness of which did not correspond with the usual effects of the poison fixed upon. As to the mark in the uterus, he gave his opinion that it might have arisen from other causes than the one alleged; two phenomena were absent, and upon this fact he asserted it to be physically impossible that there could have been a recent delivery; and, moreover, in his "Remarks," he proved mathematically that the mark was four times the size it ought to have been on that hypothesis. Miss Burns had not been attended professionally by any one as she was averse to doctors. Mr. Angus in his defence ascribed the whole of the legal proceedings against him to the malevolence of two interested parties, and had it not now been for their influence, the circumstance of Miss Burns' death would have passed over without remark. Mr. Angus, so far from desiring to harm Miss Burns, expressed himself as deeply indebted to her for her care of his children and the affection and attention to his comforts she had always manifested, and emphatically declared he "loved and respected her too well to dream of doing her any harm."

# CHAPTER VI.

When I look around and see the various changes that have taken place in this "good old town" I am sometimes lost in wonderment. Narrow, inconvenient, ill-paved streets have been succeeded by broad thoroughfares—old tumble-down houses have been replaced by handsome and costly buildings, while the poor little humble shops that once were sufficient for our wants have been completely eclipsed by the gigantic and elegant "establishments" of the present day.

I recollect Dale-street when it was a narrow thoroughfare, ill-paved and ill-lighted at night. It was not half the present width. In 1808, as the town began to spread and its traffic increase, great complaints were constantly being made of the inconvenience of the principal streets, and it was agreed on all sides that something should be done towards improvement. The first movement was made by widening Dale-street; the improvement being by throwing the thoroughfare open from Castle-street to Temple-court, but it really was not until 1820 that this street was set out in anything like a bold and handsome manner. Great difficulties were constantly thrown in the way of alterations by many of the inhabitants, who had lived in their old houses, made fortunes under their roofs, and were hoping to live and die where they had been born and brought up. Many tough battles had the authorities to fight with the owners of the property. Some were most unreasonable in the compensation they demanded, while others for a time obstinately refused to enter into any negotiations whatever, completely disregarding all promised advantages. The most obtuse and determined man was a shoemaker or cobbler, who owned a small house and shop which stood near Hockenall-alley. Nothing could persuade him to go out of his house or listen to any proposition. Out he would not go, although his neighbours had disappeared and his house actually stood like an island in the midst of the traffic current. The road was carried on each side of his house, but there stood the cobbler's stall alone in its glory. While new and comfortable dwellings were springing up, the old cobbler laughed at his persecutors, defied them, and stood his ground in spite of all entreaty. There the house stood in the middle of the street, and for a long time put a stop to further and complete improvement, until the authorities, roused by the indignation of the public, took forcible possession of the place and pulled the old obnoxious building about the owner's ears, in spite of his resistance and his fighting manfully for what he thought were his rights; nor would he leave the house until it had been unroofed, the floors torn up, and the walls crumbling and falling down from room to room. The cobbler stuck to his old house to the last, showing fight all through, with a determination and persistence worthy of a nobler cause. Some few years ago a barber, also in Dale-street, exhibited an equal degree of persistence in keeping possession of his shop which was wanted for an improvement near Temple-street. This man clung to his old house and shop until it was made utterly uninhabitable..

Dale-street, when I was a boy, was not very much broader than Sir Thomas's Buildings; in some parts it was quite as narrow, especially about Cumberland-street end. The carrying trade at one time from Liverpool was by means of packhorses, long strings of which used to leave the town with their burthens, attended by their drivers, and always mustered together in considerable number in Dale-street previous to starting. This they did that they might be strong enough to resist the highwaymen who infested the roads at the end of the last century. I have often heard my father talk of these free gentlemen's exploits, and the sometimes droll adventures arising from their presence. He used to tell a story of three volunteer officers going to Warrington by the stage to a county muster, being stopped by a pretended footpad (a friend in disguise) the other side of Prescot, and ignominiously robbed of everything they possessed, even their very swords. I cannot say I believed the story, because I felt sure no officers, whatever service they might be in, would have allowed themselves to be so treated. My father frequented the tavern which stood where Promoli's Bazaar now stands, and where all the leading tradesmen used to assemble, and he told us that the three officers were there one night and were terribly "trotted" about their losses and that they did not altogether "deny the soft impeachment." There was a good story current in Liverpool, I have been told, in 1745, touching the doings of Mr. Campbell's regiment which, when the rebellion broke out in that year, was suddenly called into active service with orders to march to Manchester, by way of Warrington, to resist a party of Scots said to be in that neighbourhood. The regiment marched at night, and of course threw out an advanced guard. When about two miles this side of Warrington, the vanguard fell back reporting that they had seen a party of the enemy bivouacking in the road about a quarter of a mile ahead, and that they could see them quite plainly lying on the ground, at the sides and in the middle of the road. A halt was called, and a council of war summoned. Hearts beat quickly in some hardy frames who boldly advised an onward march, while others were for retreating until some good plan of attack could be determined upon. Some were for diverging from the road and continuing the march through the lanes and bye-ways, so that, if necessary, the enemy could be outflanked. One bolder than the rest offered to go forward as a scout. His proposition was eagerly accepted. Away he went, and soon in the distance a terrible uproar was heard—the volunteers flew to arms, and waited in breathless suspense. They were surprised, however, to hear the alarm raised, but no shots fired. The row subsided, when presently the gallant scout was seen approaching with a prisoner he had bravely captured—in the form of a fat goose. The fact was that a flock of geese had got out into the road, and they presented an appearance to the advanced guard of troops bivouacking. The bold men of Liverpool were then led undauntedly forward, and it was said that every other man marched into Warrington with his supper on his knapsack.

The most admirable improvements that the town underwent was when Lord-street was widened and the Crescent formed, the completion of which undertaking cost upwards of half a million of money. Castle-street was narrow, badly paved, and badly lighted at night, as, indeed, was the whole town. Yet, I recollect there were some people who objected to the improvements at the top of Lord-street, who clung pertinaciously to the old Potato Market, and the block of buildings called Castle Hill. The houses that were erected upon the site of Castle Ditch had the floors of some of their rooms greatly inclined in consequence of the subsidence of the soil. There was a joke current at the time that these apartments ought to be devoted to dining purposes, as the gravy would always run to one side of the plate!

A great increase has taken place in the value of property in every part of the town. In Castle-street sixty years ago a house and shop could be had for £30 per annum. The premises in which Roscoe's Bank was carried on, and now occupied by Messrs. Nixon, were purchased by Mr. Harvey who, finding his property remaining unoccupied for so long a time, began to despair of letting it, and grew quite nervous about his bargain. On the formation of Brunswick-street, projected in 1786, this handsome thoroughfare was cut through Smock-alley and the houses in Chorley-street, and swept away a portion of the old Theatre Royal in Drury-lane; it then ran down to the old Custom-house yard, on the site of which the Goree Piazzas and warehouses were erected. Drury-lane was formerly called Entwhistle-street, after an old and influential family who filled high offices in the town in their day.

Any one can fancy what Castle-street must have been when the market was held in it, by filling Cable-street with baskets of farmers' produce, and blocking it up with all sorts of provisions and stalls, in which the usual marketable commodities would be exposed for sale.

The introduction of Gas in the town was an immense stride in the march of improvement; yet there were not a few persons who bitterly complained of the Gas Company so often disturbing the streets to enable them to lay down their pipes. Frequent letters appeared in the papers of the time to that effect. Previous to 1817 the town was wretchedly lighted by oil lamps which used to go out upon all trifling occasions and for insufficient reasons. They only pretended to show light at the best of times. The lamps were not lit in summer nor on moonlight nights. They were generally extinguished by four or five o'clock in the morning.

The gentry were at one time attended by link-men or boys in their night excursions. These links were stiff, tarred ropes about the thickness of a man's arm. They gave a flaring light with any quantity of bituminous-odoured smoke. In front of one or two of the old houses of Liverpool I have seen a remnant of the link days, in an extinguisher attached to the lamp iron. I think there is (or was) one in Mount Pleasant, near the house with the variegated pebble pavement in front (laid down, by the way, by a blind man). The link-extinguisher was a sort of narrow iron funnel of about six inches in diameter at the widest end. It was usually attached to a lamp-iron, and was used by thrusting the link up it, when the light was to be put out.

People in those days seldom went out at night without a lantern, for what with the ruggedness of the pavements and the vile state of the roads it was by no means safe to life or limb to go without some mode of illuminating the way.

Gas was introduced in 1816 and 1817. Only one side of Castle-street was lighted at first. While we now acknowledge the invaluable introduction of this fluid, when we consider the vast area over which it casts its pleasant and cheerful beams, and the price we also pay for such an unmistakable comfort and blessing, we shall not fail to peruse the first advertisement of the Gas Company with intense interest. With this belief I insert a copy of it. The rate of charge and the mode of ascertaining the quantity of light consumed cannot but prove curious to us and rather puzzling perhaps to understand.

### LIVERPOOL GAS-LIGHT COMPANY.

Scale of Charges per Annum for Burners of various sizes, calculated for lighting to the hours below mentioned:—

| One Argand. | Till 8 o'Clock. | Till 9 o'Clock. | Till 10 o'Clock. | Till 11 o'Clock. | Till 12 o'Clock. |
|---|---|---|---|---|---|
|  | £ s. d. | £ s. d. | £ s. d. | £ s. d. | £ s. d. |
| No. 1, | 3 0 0 | 3 18 0 | 4 16 0 | 5 12 0 | 6 8 0 |

| No. 2, | 2 14 0 | 3 5 0 | 4 0 0 | 4 14 0 | 5 8 0 |
| No. 3, | 2 2 0 | 2 14 0 | 3 7 0 | 3 18 0 | 4 10 0 |
| One Batwing. | 2 14 0 | 3 5 0 | 4 0 0 | 4 14 0 | 5 8 0 |

Persons who wish to take the Light, may make application at the Company's Office, Hatton-garden, where their names will be entered numerically in a Book, and Branch-pipes laid in rotation, the Company only contracting to fix the pipes just within the house, and to supply the Light when the interior is fitted up, and made air-tight and perfect, which must be done by each individual, and approved by the Company's Engineer.

No extra charge will be made, if the Light be extinguished in a quarter of an hour after the time contracted for, and on Saturday evenings the Company will allow burning till twelve o'clock.

The Rents will be collected at the commencement of each Quarter, and will be apportioned as follows: Two-thirds of the above prices for the two winter quarters, and One-third for the two summer quarters. If the Lights amount, by the above table, to £10 per annum, a Discount of 2½ per cent. will be allowed; if to £20, 5 per cent.; if to £30, 7½ per cent.; if to £40, 10 per cent.; and if to £50, 12½ per cent.

By Order of the Committee,
CHARLES ROWLINSON,
Secretary.

*6th June*, 1817.

Just fancy such a tariff to be in existence at present!

Lord-street, previous to 1827, was very narrow; it was not so wide even as Dale-street. The houses and all the streets in Liverpool were just as we see in third-rate country towns, having bowed shop-windows, or square ones, projecting from the side of the house. I recollect Church-street and Ranelagh-street being paved in the centre only. Cable-street, Redcross-street and Park-lane were only flagged in 1821; and nearly all the houses in these streets were then private dwellings. In Ranelagh-street the houses had high steps to the front doors. The porches of the old houses in Liverpool were remarkable for their handsome appearance and patterns. Many still remain but they are yearly decreasing in number. I recollect when the only shops in Church-street were a grocer's (where part of Compton House now stands) and a confectioner's at the corner of Church-alley. Bold-street was nearly all private houses, and there were very few shops in it, even some forty years ago. Seventy years since there was scarcely a house of any sort in it. I have been told that where the Athenæum now stands in Church-street, there was once a large pond on which the skaters used to cut a figure, and that a farm-house stood at the corner of Hanover-street. Some houses in Hanover-street will be noticed as being built out at angles with the street. This was to secure a good view of the river from the windows. At the corner of Bold-street some ninety years ago was a milkman's cottage and dairy. Whitechapel, when I was a lad, was a dreadful thoroughfare. I have seen it deep in water, and boats rowed about, conveying people from house to house, in times of flood. There used to be a channel with water running down the centre of the street, which was considerably lower than it is at present. It was no uncommon thing for the cellars of all the houses to be filled with water, and even now, I believe, some portion of the neighbourhood is not unfrequently rendered damp and uncomfortable. In the cellars under the Forum, in Marble-street, there is a very deep well which is at all times full; this well drains the premises. This Forum, about fifty years ago, was a well-known and much frequented arena for disputations of all sorts. Many a clever speaker has addressed audiences now passed away. Speaker and spoken to are for the most part gone. A great change took place some forty years ago in the locality where St. John's Market now stands. There was a ropewalk here which extended from where the angle of the building faces the Amphitheatre, as far as Renshaw-street. There was a field at one time to the north of the ropery skirted by hedges which went down the site of the present Hood-street, and round to where there is now a large draper's shop in the Old Haymarket; the hedge then went up John's-lane, and so round by the site of the lamp opposite the Queen's Hotel, along Limekiln-lane to Ranelagh-street. These were all fields, being a portion of what was anciently called "the Great Heath." It was at one time intended to erect a handsome Crescent where the cab-stand is now. The almshouses stood on this ground. Limekiln-lane, now Lime-street, was so called from the limekiln that stood on the site of the present Skelhorn-street. Here were open fields, which extended to the London-road, quite famous for the assembling of all sorts of rough characters, especially on summer evenings, and on Sundays. Cock-fighting, dog-fighting, and pugilistic encounters used to be carried on daily, and scenes of the utmost confusion took place, until public murmurings compelled the authorities to keep order. It was in the fields about where the Lord Nelson-street rooms stand, that my grandfather recollects seeing three, if not four, men hung for being mixed up in the rebellion of '45. They were hung there in chains for some time, and afterwards buried at the foot of the gallows as a warning to evil-doers.

There were several mills in this vicinity, one of which was called the White Mill, and there was a very curious story once commonly current about it, in the town to the effect that the owner of it had been murdered by a friend of his who kept a mill lower down the hill. Whitemill-street is called after this White Mill. The lower mill stood where Hotham-street is now, which formerly was called Duncan-street. The mill occupied the site of the Quaker's school, which was pulled down to make room for the railway yard. When this mill was razed to the ground, a grave was discovered in the foundation, in which was a skeleton, and it was freely said that this was the White Mill miller, who had so mysteriously disappeared some years previously. It was the talk of the town at the time, and crowds of persons went to the spot to look at the grave. When the mill in Duncan-street was taken down it was so rotten that it was razed to the ground in one day. Where St. George's Hall now stands was the Infirmary. It faced Islington Triangle, afterwards converted into a market-place, being built round with small shops, having a pump in the middle. When this market was discontinued in 1848, the tenants were removed to Gill-street, on its opening in September of that year. The Infirmary consisted of two wings and a centre; at the back was a spacious garden or airing ground. On Shaw's Brow lived the potters. There were upwards of 2,000 persons engaged in this trade, which was carried on to a very great extent. Pottery in Liverpool was a considerable manufacture, and it is said that it was Mr. Sadler, a potter who lived in Harrington-street, that first discovered the art of printing upon earthenware, through seeing his children stick pieces of printed cotton fabric on some damaged plates they were playing with. There were many other large potteries in Liverpool at one period, besides those on Shaw's Brow. There was one at the corner of Fontenoy-street, of which Alderman Shaw was proprietor. There was one at the bottom of Duke-street. This was kept by Mr. Drinkwater, who married Captain Leece's daughter, after whom Leece-street is named. Pothouse-lane is a reminder of the old trade. There were other potteries on Copperas-hill. I do not recollect much about these potteries; but I have heard my father and mother talk about them amongst their "Recollections." This trade seems to have departed from this town most strangely. The last remnant of it was in the works that were in operation down by the river-side near the present Toxteth Docks. Watch-making has always been a great trade in Liverpool. The first introducer of it was Mr. Wyke, who lived in Dale-street, on the site of the present public offices. Mr. Wyke came from Prescot, and carried on a large trade in watches about the year 1758. Mr. Litherland, the inventor of the chronometer, died in Church-street. On Mr. Wyke's premises and garden the Gas Works were afterwards erected, which were removed to Newington some few years ago. Amongst many others I have seen some very remarkable changes that have taken place about Bevington-hill. I recollect very well what is now called "Summer Seat" being gardens, and the view from them to the river quite uninterrupted. There was near them a house built by a shoemaker who had made a fortune by his trade; it was called "Lapstone Hall." The inn called the "Bush" had a bough hanging out with the motto "Good Wine Needs no Bush." The sailors were very fond of going up to Bevington-Bush on Sundays with their sweethearts, and many a boisterous scene have I witnessed there. The view was really beautiful from the gardens. Where the market stands in Scotland-road there used to be a large stone quarry. The houses in Scotland-road beyond the market are all of very late erection. I can well recollect open fields and market gardens thereabouts, and, indeed, all the way up where Scotland-road now is, there used to be fields. The Preston-road wound round up Bevington-Bush. The Everton range looked very pretty from the Kirkdale-road, especially when handsome mansions began to dot its crest. I recollect along this road cornfields, meadows and gardens. Scotland-road is a comparatively newly-formed thoroughfare. Any one turning to the left at the bottom of Scotland-road, and going to Bevington-Bush will see, in those old houses on the right hand, of what Liverpool, in my young days, was composed. Very few specimens of the old town houses are now remaining, so speedily do they become modernized and altered. I like those quaint old buildings although they were not very comfortable within, from their narrow windows and low ceilings, but there has been a great deal of mirth and jollity in some of those old low-roofed houses in the town, in our great privateering and slave-dealing times.

I have often heard old people talk about *their* "Recollections" of the town. I have heard them speak of Clayton-square being laid out in the memorable year of 1745. Mrs. or Madame Clayton to whose family this part of the town chiefly belonged, was the daughter of Mr. Clayton who was Mayor in 1689, and who represented the town in parliament for eight sessions. Madame Clayton's house stood near Cases-street. Her garden was said to have been the best kept and most productive in the town. It was this lady who started the first private carriage in Liverpool. I have heard it said that people used to stare at it, as if it was something wonderful. The streets about Church-street are all called after the old families. Parker-street was called after Mr. Parker, of Cuerdon, who married Miss Ann Clayton. Their daughter Jane married one of the Tarletons. Tarleton-street is named after Colonel Banastre Tarleton. Banastre-street is named after him also. Houghton-street is after the old Houghton family. Williamson-square was laid out in 1745 by Mr.

Williamson. Basnett-street was called after the Basnetts, at one time a very influential family of old Liverpool; Leigh-street after the Leighs; Cases-street after the Cases. Mr. Rose, who projected many streets at the north end of the town on his extensive property, seems to have adopted the poets' names to distinguish his thoroughfares, as in Chaucer, Ben Jonson, Juvenal, Virgil, Dryden, Milton, Sawney (Alexander) Pope-street, etc. Meadows-street, Scotland-road, was named after Mr. William Meadows, who married six wives. His first wife lived two years. He next married Peggy Robinson, who lived twenty years, and bore him children; after being a widower a month, he again married. This wife lived two years. After remaining a widower seven weeks, he married his fourth wife, who lived eighteen years. After a nine months' single blessedness he again married. After his fifth wife's death he remained a widower thirty-four weeks, and at the age of seventy-five, on the 10th of June, 1807, he married Miss Ann Lowe, of Preston-street. William Meadows was thought to be a bold man. Maguire-street was named after Mr. Maguire who kept a shop in Lord-street. Benson-street was called after Moses Benson, Esq. Bixteth-street after Alderman Bixteth, who is said "to have been publicly thanked by the authorities for paving the front of his house with his own hands." Pudsey-street after Pudsey Dawson. Seel-street after Mr. Seel, who lived at the corner of it. Wolstenholme-square and street, after an influential family of that name. Bold-street after the Bolds, who built the first house in it: now occupied by Mr. Dismore. Colquitt-street after the Colquitts, whose mansion was converted into the Royal Institution. Berry-street, was named after Captain Berry, who built the first house at the corner of Bold-street. Cropper-street after the Cropper family. Fazakerly-street after the Fazakerlys. Oakes-street after Captain Oakes, who died in 1808. Lydia Ann-street after Mademoiselle Lydia Ann De La Croix, who married Mr. Perry, the originator of Fawcett's foundry, and the Coal Brook Dale iron works. Mason-street, Edge-hill, was named after Mr. Mason, who built and endowed Edge-hill church, and whose mansion stood at the corner of Mason-street, the gardens of which extended to the bottom of Paddington. James-street was named after Mr. Roger James, who held large property in it. Preeson's-row was named after Alderman Preeson, who built his house and two others of the old Castle materials. Part of Castle-street is also constructed of the timbers and stones. Old Peter-street which ran out of School-lane has disappeared. Crosshall-street was called after the Hall and gardens of the Crosses which stood on the site of (or about) Manchester-street. Part of Fenwick-street was called Dry Bridge, a bridge passing over the Old Ropery, the name of which is perpetuated in that street. Holden's Weint was re-named Brook-street. Lower Stanley-street was re-named Button-street, after Mr. Button, who lived to a great age, and saw I don't know how many king's reigns. The streets of Liverpool seem to have been named, in some parts of the town, as it were, in classes, as I have mentioned. Mr. Rose called his new thoroughfares after the poets, and in another neighbourhood we find the names of celebrated commanders affording street-titles as in Blake-street, Duncan-street (afterwards Hotham-street), Clarence-street, Russell-street, Rodney-street, Seymour-street, Rupert-street, etc. While on the site of the old Botanic Gardens at the top of Oxford-street, we find Laurel-street, Grove-street, Oak, Vine, and Myrtle-streets. In Kensington, on the site of Dr. Solomon's property, we have streets named after celebrated lawyers, and this locality is jocosely called "Judge's Land." We have streets thereabout bearing the names of Cottenham, Coltman, Wightman, Patteson, Pollock, and Coleridge, and there may also be found a Gilead and a Solomon-street.

By the way, a reference to Dr. Solomon's property, at Kensington, reminds me of the good stories that were current in Liverpool about the worthy doctor himself. I recollect one wherein the laugh was loud at the Custom-house authorities, who had been nicely bitten by a seizure they had made of some of the doctor's "exports." It was said that a quantity of "Balm of Gilead," upon which drawback was claimed, had been seized by the Custom-house people as not being of the specified value to entitle Dr. Solomon to claim so large an amount of drawback. The doctor was, as may be supposed, very wrath at his "goots" being waylaid, but he determined upon revenge. Making up a lot of sugar and water, well-flavoured with spice, the doctor entered a large case "outward," declaring it to be of the same value as the former seized case. The trap fell, and the Custom-house authorities were caught, to the intense satisfaction of the doctor, who told them he "vould teach them to seize his goots!"

Another story is told of the doctor once entertaining a party of gentlemen at Gilead House (as was often his custom), and towards the close of the evening, some one began joking the doctor about his "Balm of Gilead." The doctor bore the jesting very well, and on being told he ought to let those present taste it, readily consented to open a few bottles. Now this Balm, I believe, was very good, and was made, it was said, of strong alcohol or brandy, and the richest spices. The bottles of "Balm" passed round and were duly appreciated. On the guests preparing to leave, they were presented with "a little bill" amounting to about a guinea each for the Balm of Gilead which had been consumed. The doctor telling them that it was by means of the "Balm" he lived, and through the "Balm" he was enabled to invite them to partake of his really bountiful hospitality. Each guest paid his bill, admitting that the doctor was right, and that they had merited the reproof so properly administered to them.

The doctor used to drive a handsome team of four horses, and, of course, attracted a good deal of attention whenever he made his appearance in the streets. On one occasion the late Lord Sefton, who was through life a first-rate whip, drove up to Heywood's bank in his usual dashing style. Dr. Solomon was tooling along behind his lordship, and desirous of emulating his mode of handling the reins and whip, gave the latter such a flourish as to get the lash so firmly fixed round his neck as to require his groom's aid to release him from its folds.

I will now give the derivations of a few more streets, as I have heard them spoken of by old people; they may be interesting to my readers: Benn's Gardens was called after Mr. Benn, who was bailiff, in 1697. He resided in Pool-lane, now South Castle-street; his garden occupied this locality. Atherton-street was named after Mr. Peter Atherton, who was bailiff, in 1673. Bird-street was named after Mr. Joseph Bird, who was bailiff, in 1738; mayor in 1746. In Birch-field resided Mr. Birch. Roscoe lived here at one time, and it was here he wrote the greater part of the lives of "The Medici." I recollect a great many fine trees being in and about this vicinity. Bolton-street was named after John Bolton, Esq., or Colonel Bolton as he was called. Byrom-street was named after Octavius Byrom. Chisenhale-street is named after Chisenhale Johnson. Chorley-street is called after Mr. Chorley, who was recorder of Liverpool from 1602 till 1620. Canning-street is named in honour of the statesman. Cleveland-square takes its name from the Clevelands; it was formerly called Price-square. The Prices were lords of the manor of Birkenhead. Gildart Garden is named after Mr. Gildart, who was bailiff in 1712, and mayor in 1714, 1731, and 1736. Gill-street is named after Mr. Gill, who owned the land thereabouts. Harrington-street is called after the Harrington family, who once held considerable property in Liverpool. Hackin's-hey is called after John Hackin, who was a tenant of the More's of olden time. Huskisson-street is named after the statesman at one time member for Liverpool. Cresswell-street after Sir Cresswell Cresswell, also an ex-borough member. Brougham-terrace, after Lord Brougham. Hockenhall-alley is called after a very old Liverpool family. Lord-street is named after Lord Molyneux. Redcross-street was so named in consequence of a red obelisk which stood in the open ground, south of St. George's Church. This street was originally called Tarleton's New-street. Shaw-street was named after "Squire Shaw," who held much property at Everton. Sir Thomas's Buildings is called after Sir Thomas Johnson, who, when Mayor, benevolently caused St. James's Mount to be erected as a means of employing the destitute poor in the severe winter of 1767. Strand-street derived its name from being the strand or shore of the river. Hunter-street and South Hunter-street, Maryland-street, Baltimore-street, etc., were named after Mr. John Hunter, an eminent merchant trading with the States, who dwelt in Mount Pleasant, and whose gardens extended to Rodney-street.

# CHAPTER VII.

In 1801, my wife being out of health, I was advised to take her from town. As Everton was recommended by Dr. Parks, I looked about in that neighbourhood, and after some difficulty obtained accommodation in a neat farm-house which stood on the rise of the hill. I say it was with difficulty that I could meet with the rooms I required, or any rooms at all, for there were so few houses at Everton, and the occupants of them so independent, that they seemed loth to receive lodgers on any terms. It must appear strange to find Everton spoken of as being "out of town," but it was literally so then. It was, comparatively speaking, as much so as West Derby, or any of the neighbouring villages round Liverpool, are at present.

The farm-house in which we resided has long since been swept away, with its barns, its piggery, and its shippon. Never more will its cornricks gladden the eye—never more will busy agricultural life be carried on in its precincts. Streets and courts full of houses cumber the ground. No more will the lark be heard over the cornfield—the brook seen running its silvery course—or the apple in the orchard reddening on the bending bough. The lark is represented by a canary in a gilded cage hanging out of a first-floor window—the corn-field by the baker's shop, with flour at eight pounds for a shilling—the brook is a sewer, and the apple is only seen at the greengrocer's shop at the corner, in company with American cheese, eggs, finnon-haddies, and lucifer matches. Ditch and hedge—the one with waving sedges and "Forget-me-nots" the other with the May blossom loading the evening air with its balmy breath—were as prevalent, at the time I speak about, in Everton, as you will now find in any country district. It was a pleasant place in summer and autumn time. The neighbourhood of the Beacon was our favourite resort. Many a pleasant day we have spent at the top of it. The hill was covered with heather and gorse bushes. In winter it was as wild, bleak, and cold a place as any you could meet with.

In the summer it was the delight of holiday-makers. A day's "out" to the Beacon, at Everton, was a very favourite excursion. The hill-side on Sundays used to be thronged with merry people, old and young. The view obtained from Everton Beacon-hill was a view indeed.

And what a prospect! What a noble panoramic scene! I never saw its like. I do not think, in its way, such an one existed anywhere to be compared with it. At your feet the heather commenced the landscape, then came golden corn-fields and green pasture-lands, far and wide, until they reached the yellow undulating sand-hills that fringed the margin of the broad estuary, the sparkling waters of which, in the glow and fulness of the rich sunshine, gave life and animation to the scene, the interest of which was deeply enhanced, when on a day of high-tide, numbers of vessels might be seen spreading their snowy canvas in the wind as they set out on their distant and perilous voyages. In the middle ground of the picture was the peninsula of Wirral, while the river Dee might be seen shimmering like a silver thread under the blue hills of Wales, which occupied the back ground of the landscape. Westward was the ocean—next, the Formby shore attracted the eye. The sand-hills about Birkdale and Meols were visible. At certain seasons, and in peculiar states of the atmosphere, the hummocks of the Isle of Man were to be seen, while further north Black Combe, in Cumberland, was discernible. Bleasdale Scar, and the hills in Westmoreland, dimly made out the extreme distance. Ashurst Beacon, Billinge, and at their back Rivington-pike, were visible. Carrying the eye along the Billinge range, there were Garswood-park, Knowsley and Prescot; the smoke from the little town of St. Helen's might have been seen behind them. Far away to the eastward were the Derbyshire-hills. Then we saw those of Shropshire, until the eye rested on the Chester ranges, Beeston and Halton Castles being plainly before us. The old city of Chester was discernible with a good glass. The eye moved then along the Welsh hills until it rested on the Ormeshead and travelled out upon the North sea. Below us, to our left, was the town of Liverpool, the young giant just springing into vigorous life and preparing to put forth its might, majesty and strength, in Trade, Commerce, and Enterprise. The man of 1801 can scarcely believe his eyes in 1862. The distant view is still there, from the top of Everton church tower, but how wonderfully is all the foreground changed.

The Beacon stood on the site of the eastern corner of Everton church. It was a square tower of two stories, and approached from the present Church-street by a little lane. Church-street was then a sandy winding road, having on one side the open heathery-hill, and on the other a low turf wall which enclosed the fields called "the Mosses," which were indeed little better than marshes. The Beacon was constructed of the red sandstone taken from the vicinity. I am no antiquarian, so that I can give but a poor opinion of its original date of erection. It was said by some to have been of great age—long previous to the time of Queen Elizabeth. Some even ascribed it to the time of the Earl of Chester; but a learned friend of mine once told me, when talking on this subject, that that could not have been the case, as Beacons were not erected in tower shapes until after the time of Edward the Third.

Beacons, previously to that period, were merely lighted fires in cressets, grates, baskets of large size, or of faggots piled up. Everton Beacon certainly looked very old and dilapidated, and had stood the shock and buffet of some centuries. Its size was about six yards square; its height twenty-five feet. The basement floor was on a level with the ground, and was a square room in which there was, in one corner, a fireplace, much knocked about and broken. There was also a flight of narrow stone steps which led to the upper chamber. It was utterly bare of any fittings whatever; but in the walls were indications of there having been fixtures at some time. There being no door to it the cattle which grazed on the hill had access to it at all times of storm or wind or heat, or as their bovine inclinations should prompt them to seek shelter, so that the floor, which was unflagged, was always in a very dirty state. On ascending the stairs access was obtained to the upper apartment which was lighted by a broad window facing the westward. This room had been used as a sleeping apartment by the guard or custodian of the Beacon, the window serving as a look-out. I believe the combustibles used in lighting up the signals were stored in it, the lower room being occupied as the common living chamber. From the upper room a flight of stone steps led upon the roof or outer platform. In the south-west corner was a large stone tank in which the signal fires were lighted. It seemed to have been subjected to the action of intense heat. At one corner was a sort of pent-house which served as a shelter for the watchman in inclement weather. On the east wall a gooseberry bush flourished surprisingly. How it came there no one knew—it had long been remembered in that position by every one who knew anything about the Tower. A few years previous to the date I speak about, the Beacon was occupied by a cobbler who carried on his trade in it, and eked out a living by grazing a cow and some goats on the common land in the vicinity. He looked after them while he made, mended, or cobbled. It was a very current tradition in Everton that during the early part of the reign of Charles the First, people came up to Everton Beacon to be married, during the proscription of the clergy. When Thurot's expedition was expected in 1760, it was said that Everton Hill was alive with people from the town waiting the freebooters' approach. A party of soldiers was then encamped on the hill, and I have been told the men had orders, on Thurot's appearance, to make signals if by day, and to light up the Beacon if at night, to communicate the intelligence of the French fleet being off the coast to the other Beacons at Ashurst and Billinge, Rivington-pike and elsewhere, and so spread the news into the north; while signals would also be taken up at Halton, Beeston, the Wreken, and thence to the southward. The most perfect arrangements for the transmission of this intelligence are said to have been made; and I knew an old man at Everton who told me that he had on that occasion carted several loads of pitch-barrels and turpentine and stored them in the upper chamber of the Beacon to be ready in case of emergency. He said that during the French war, at the close of the reign of George the Second, the Beacon was filled with combustibles, and that there was a guard always kept therein.

I am not sure if it is very generally known that it was to a Liverpool captain the discovery of the sailing of the Armada must be ascribed, and through him was made public in England. This captain's name was Humphrey Brook. He was outward bound from Liverpool to the Canaries when he saw the Spanish fleet in the distance, sailing north. Suspecting its errand he put his helm up and hastened back to Plymouth, where he spread the intelligence and caused it to be transmitted to London. He received substantial marks of favour from the Government for his foresight, prudence, and activity.

In 1804 a telegraph station was established at Everton. It stood where the schools are now built. It was discontinued in 1815. It consisted of an upright post whence arms extended at various angles—there was also a tall flag-staff for signals. While we were at Everton, a Mr. Hinde erected a house at the corner of Priory-lane, which he intended should represent the Beacon; but it was not a bit like it originally, nor at the present time (for I believe the house is still standing). Mr. Hinde had not long erected his Tower before he found that it was giving way. To prevent it falling he ran up a wing to the westward. He then found that it was necessary to erect a southern wing to keep that side up also. Hence the present appearance of the house which has always been a subject of wonder and remark by strangers at its eccentric and unusual aspect.

I recollect St. Domingo Pit being much more extensive than it has been of late years. At one period it was fully one-third larger than it is now. Those large stones that stand by its brink are the "Mere Stones." There were several more stones about which marked Everton's ancient boundaries. There was one, I recollect, in the West Derby-road, near the Zoological Gardens. I often wonder if this relic of the past has been preserved. A branch of the Pool ran up the westward and formed an ornamental water in the grounds that skirted the Pool, a rustic bridge being thrown over it. The cottage at one corner of the Pool is the ancient pinfold, and the rent of it was paid to the lord of the manor. The view from this part of Everton was very fine before houses began to spring up in its vicinity. I do not know a finer prospect anywhere about Liverpool. When we were staying at Everton there were very few houses. I dare say there were not fifty houses in the whole district, and the inhabitants did not muster more than 400 souls; and it was not until 1818 or 1820 that much increase took place in its population.

# CHAPTER VIII.

In 1820, a rather curious circumstance transpired, which created a good deal of conversation, and even consternation amongst the inhabitants of Everton. This was the extraordinary and mysterious disappearance of the Cross which stood at the top of the village, a little to the westward of where the present Everton road is lineable with Everton-lodge. This Cross was a round pillar, about four feet from the top of three square stone steps. On the apex of the column was a sun-dial. This Cross had long been pronounced a nuisance; and fervent were the wishes for its removal by those who had to travel that road on a dark night, as frequent collisions took place from its being so much in the way of the traffic. When any one, however, spoke of its removal, the old inhabitants so strongly protested against its being touched, that the authorities gave up all hope of ever overcoming the prejudice in favour of its remaining. However, a serious accident having occurred, it was at length determined by the late Sir William Shaw, to do what others dared not. One dark and stormy winter's night, when all Everton was at rest—for there were no old watchmen then to wake people up with their cries—two persons might have been seen stealing towards the Cross, in the midst of the elemental war which then raged. One of them bore a lantern, while the other wheeled before him a barrow, laden with crowbar, pickaxe, and spade. The rain descended in torrents, and the night was as dark as the deed they were about to commit could possibly require. They approached the ancient gathering place, where, in olden times, during the sweating sickness, the people from Liverpool met the farmers of the district and there paid for all produce by depositing their money in bowls of water. Amidst the storm the two men for a moment surveyed their stony victim, and then commenced its destruction. First, with a strong effort, they toppled over the upper stone of the column; then the next, and the next. They then wheeled them away, stone by stone, to the Round House on Everton-brow, wherein each fragment was deposited. The base was then ruthlessly removed and carried away, and at length not a vestige was left to mark the spot where once stood Everton Cross—raised doubtless by pious hands on some remarkable occasion long forgotten.

The Cross was thus safely housed and stored away in the Round House, and no one was the wiser. When morning dawned the astonishment of the early Everton birds was extreme. From house to house—few in number, then—ran the news that Everton Cross had disappeared during the storm of the previous night. The inhabitants soon mustered on the spot, and deep and long and loud were the lamentations uttered at its removal. Who did it? When? How? At length a whisper was passed from mouth to mouth—at first faintly and scarcely intelligible—until, gathering strength as it travelled, it became at length boldly asserted that the Father of Lies had taken it away in the turbulence of the elements. And so the news spread through Liverpool, in the year 1820, that the Devil had run off with the Cross at Everton. My old friend, who many a time chuckled over his feat, and who told me of his doings, said that for many years he feared to tell the truth about it, so indignant were many of the inhabitants who knew that its disappearance could not have been attributable to satanic agency. My friend used to say that he had hard work to preserve his gravity when listening to the various versions that were prevalent of the circumstance.

Opposite the Cross there were some very old houses of the same type, character, and date as that known as Prince Rupert's cottage. The latter was a low long building, constructed of stone, lath, and plaster, and presented the appearance of an ordinary country cottage. Prince Rupert's officers were quartered in the village houses. At the back of the cottage, Rupert constructed his first battery. It was a square platform, and was used as a garden, until cottage and all were swept away for the new streets now to be found thereabouts. I can recollect the whole of the land from Everton Village to Brunswick Road being pasture land, and Mr. Plumpton's five houses in Everton Road, overlooking the fields, commanded high rents when first erected. Low-hill at this time was a rough, sandy, undulating lane with hedges on both sides. The only dwellings in it were a large house near the West Derby-road, and two low cottages opposite Phythian-street, still standing. The public-house at the corner of Low-hill and the Prescot-road is of considerable antiquity, there having been a tavern at this spot from almost all time, so to speak. Hall-lane was then called Cheetham's-brow.

Amongst other objects of interest that have disappeared at Everton, may be numbered "Gregson's Well," which stood on the left hand side of the gateway of Mr. Gregson's mansion. This well, before water was brought into our town in such abundance, was a great resort for the matrons, maids, and children of the neighbourhood, and slaked the thirst of many a weary traveller. It was a fine spring of water, and was approached by stone steps: the water issuing from a recess in the wall. "Gregson's Well" was a known trysting-place. There was an iron railing which enclosed the side and ends of the well, to prevent accidents. The water from the well is still flowing, I have been told. The stream runs underground, behind the houses in

Brunswick-road—or, at least, it did so a few years ago. I have seen the bed of the stream that ran in the olden time down Moss-street, laid open many times when the road has been taken up. There was a curious story once current about the way that Brunswick-road obtained its name. It is said that when the new streets in that vicinity were being laid out and named, the original appellation which it bore, was chalked up as copy for the painter; but a patriotic lady, during the absence of the workman rubbed out the old name and substituted for it "Brunswick-road," which name it has ever since borne.

Where Mr. Gregson's house stood, or nearly so, there was a house which, in the early part of the last century, belonged to a gentleman and his sister named Fabius. Their real name was Bean; but, after the manner of the then learned, they assumed the name of Fabius, from "Faba." Mr. or, as he was called, "Dr." Fabius was an apothecary, and received brevet rank—I suppose from being the only medical practitioner about. At any rate, from the limited population of the vicinity, he was doubtless sufficient for its wants. This Mr. Fabius was one of the first Baptists in this part of the country, and in 1700 obtained a license from Manchester, to use a room in his house as a prayer-room for that particular class of worshippers. Mr. Fabius and his sister Hanna built, after a short time, a chapel or tabernacle of wood, in their garden, and gave to the Baptists "for ever" the "piece of land adjoining the chapel-field," as a burying-place; and in this little cemetery have all the earliest leading members of this influential body been interred. It has been quite full for some years, and in consequence the Necropolis Cemetery sprung as it were from it, where dissenters of all denominations could be buried. The Baptists, increasing in numbers, quitted Low-hill, and built a chapel in Byrom-street, which is now St. Matthew's church. When this chapel was built it was thought to be too far out of town to be well attended.

There once lived a curious person at Low-hill who had peculiar tastes. He built a place which was called "Rat's Castle." It stood on the brink of a delf, the site of which is now occupied by the Prescot-street Bridewell. This person used to try experiments with food, such as cooking spiders, blackbeetles, rats, cats, mice, and other things not in common use; and, it is said, was wont to play off tricks upon unsuspecting strangers by placing banquets before them that were quite unexpected and unprecedented in the nature and condition of the food.

While lingering over my "Recollections" of Everton, I ought not to forget mentioning that, as time went on and Liverpool became prosperous, and its merchants desired to get away from the dull town-houses and imbibe healthy, fresh air, this same Everton became quite the fashionable suburb and court-end of Liverpool. Noble mansions sprung up, surrounded by well-kept gardens. Gradually the gorse-bush and the heather disappeared, and the best sites on the hill became occupied. The Everton gentry for their wealth and their pride were called "Nobles," and highly and proudly did they hold up their heads, and great state did many of the merchants who dwelt there keep up. The first mansion erected was on the Pilgrim Estate; the next was St. Domingo House. A brief history of these estates may not be uninteresting. In 1790 the whole of Everton hereabouts was owned by two proprietors. When Everton was all open, waste, and uncultivated land, one portion of it was enclosed by a shoemaker who called his acquisition "Cobbler's Close." This property was bought by Mr. Barton, who realized upwards of £190,000 through the capture of a French vessel called *La Liberte*, by a vessel owned by Joseph Birch, Esq., M.P., called *The Pilgrim*. The estate of Cobblers' Close was then re-named "Pilgrim." The property next passed into the hands of Sir William Barton, who sold it to Mr. Atherton. It was this gentleman who gave the land on which Everton Church is built, with this stipulation only—that no funerals should enter by the West Gate. The reason assigned for this was because Mr. Atherton's house was opposite to it.

Mr. Woodhouse purchased the Pilgrim estate from Mr. Atherton, and re-named it "Bronté,", from his connection with the Bronté estate in Sicily, which had been bestowed on Lord Nelson for his great services. When Lord Nelson received his first consignment of Marsala wines ordered for the fleet from his estate, he was asked to give the wine a name so that it might be known to the English people. Nelson said "call it Bronté." His lordship was told that "Bronté" meant "thunder." "Oh," replied the hero, "it will do very well; John Bull will not know what it means, and will think all the better of it on that account."

The St. Domingo Estate, in this vicinity, was originated by Mr. Campbell, who in 1757 purchased the estate. He continually added to it, as occasion presented, and called the whole "St. Domingo," in consequence of a rich prize taken by a privateer which he owned when off that island. These two contiguous estates may be said, therefore, to have been purchased by English bravery.

Mr. Crosbie was the next proprietor. He purchased it for £3500, paying £680 as deposit money. On his becoming bankrupt the estate was again put up for sale. It remained some time on hand, until Messrs. Gregson, Bridge and Parke purchased it for £4129. They sold it for £3470, losing thereby. In 1793, Mr. Sparling, who was Mayor of Liverpool in 1790, bought it. He took down the house built by Mr. Campbell and erected the handsome mansion now standing. This gentleman stipulated in his will that the house should be only occupied by a person of the name of Sparling, and that it was not to be let to any person for longer than seven years. In 1810 the legatees got the will reversed by an act of Parliament. The Queen's Dock was projected by Mr. Sparling, and Sparling-Street was called after him. The St. Domingo Estate was next sold for £20,295. It was afterwards resold for £26,383, and used as barracks.

The objections made by the people of Everton to barracks being formed in their neighbourhood were very great. A strong memorial was numerously signed by the inhabitants against the movement. The memorialists represented the demoralization attendant upon the introduction of numbers of soldiers into a respectable and quiet neighbourhood, and the annoyances that would have to be endured. But the prayer failed, and St. Domingo House, for a time, became barracks accordingly. Everton appears always to have been a favourite locality for the quartering of soldiery, when it has been necessary or expedient to station them in the vicinity of Liverpool. On several occasions entire regiments have been quartered at Everton.

The encampment of soldiers in the fields near Church-street, which a few years ago attracted great attention and curiosity, is of too recent occurrence to require remark from me, as also the occupancy of the large houses on Everton-terrace and in Waterhouse-lane and Rupert-lane by officers and men. As of old, the inhabitants of the present day sent up a remonstrance to the authorities at the Horse Guards, against soldiers being located in the neighbourhood, but with the same want of success. A most intolerable nuisance, amongst others, entailed upon the inhabitants was the beating of what, in military parlance, is called "the Daddy Mammy." This dreadful infliction upon light sleepers and invalids consisted of half a dozen boys at military daybreak (that is, as soon as you can see a white horse a mile off) learning to beat the drum. The little wretches used to batter away in Mr. Waterhouse's garden and Rupert-lane half the day through, until several letters appeared in the newspapers on the subject, which excited the wrath of the commanding officer of the regiment then stationed there, who vowed vengeance on all civilians daring to interfere with, or comment on, the rules of the service.

The Breck-road, and indeed all the roads about Everton were, but a few years back, mere country lanes, along which little passed except the farmers. There was no traffic on them as there was no leading thoroughfare to any place in the neighbourhood of the least importance. It is only within the last ten years that Everton can be said to have been at all populous. It was in my young days out by Breck-road and Anfield (originally called Hangfield), Whitefield-lane, and Roundhill-lane, completely open country. On Breck-road or Lane the only house was that at the corner of Breckfield-road, called the "Odd House." It was then a farm.

Connected with Whitefield-lane I recollect a good story told by a gentleman I knew, of his getting a free ride to Liverpool, behind the carriage of a well-known eccentric and most benevolent gentleman, some thirty years ago. My young friend who was then but lately come to Liverpool, had been invited to spend Sunday at Whitefield House, which stands at the corner of Whitefield-lane and Boundary-lane. At that time there was not a house near it for some distance. Boundary-lane was a narrow, rutted road, with a hedge and a ditch on each side, while the footpath—on one side only—was in a most miserable condition. There was then adjoining West Derby-road a large strawberry garden, which in summer time was the resort of pleasure-seekers, and it was the only approach to neighbourship along the whole length of the lane.

On leaving Whitefield House the night proved so intensely dark that my young friend found himself quite bewildered, and scarcely know whether to turn to the right or the left, being unacquainted with the locality. Fortunately turning to the right, he stumbled along the miserable road, and with the utmost difficulty made his way onward, but not without misgivings of being knocked down and robbed, as there had been several daring attacks made upon people at night in that vicinity. He fervently wished himself in Liverpool, but shortly arriving at the West Derby-road he began to understand his "whereabouts." Having proceeded a few yards, a carriage passed him driven by a postilion. There was an unoccupied dicky behind, which my young friend thought it seemed a pity not to appropriate. Quick as youth and activity prompted, he climbed upon the carriage with the notion of the Dutchman "that it was better to ride than walk," and found his condition materially benefited by being carried through the darkness of the night instead of walking. When the carriage reached the London-road my friend thought it was time to alight, as he was then near home; but to his dismay he found that, although it was very easy to get up, it was not very easy to get down in safety. On he went with the carriage until it arrived at Lime-street, and began to turn down Roe-street, which was a good mile from my friend's lodgings. What was to be done? A bold thought struck him. "Hallo, hallo! I'll get down here!" he cried. Upon this the postilion pulled up short, when down came the window of the carriage, and an inquiry from it took place as to the reason of the stoppage. My friend had by this time managed to drop off his perch, when he found the head protruding was that of the excellent lessee of the Theatre Royal, Mr. Lewis. As he was quite as polite a man as the worthy lessee himself, on finding to whom he had been indebted for his ride, he made a very low bow, with thanks for his most welcome "lift," exclaiming with Buckingham, "I will remember that your Grace is bountiful." In very sharp tones "John" was told to drive on, while my friend walked away, quietly laughing in his sleeve at the success of his impudence, but regretting that he had not alighted sooner to be nearer home.

Surprising are the changes that have taken place on the West Derby-road of late years. It was originally called Rake-lane, and Rocky-lane from Richmond-hill. A complete little town has sprung up upon its pleasant meadows and bountiful cornfields. The Zoological Gardens, within a very few years, was the uttermost verge of this suburb. I recollect very well the opening of those once beautiful gardens. They were projected by the late Mr. Atkins, a gentleman who was the proprietor of the largest travelling-menagerie in the country. The place he had selected for his undertaking was called "Plumpton's Hollow." This was originally a large excavation, whence brick-clay which abounds in the neighbourhood had been obtained. Mr. Atkins, possessing great taste and judgment, was highly favoured and much thought of by the late Lord Derby, who consulted him on many occasions and honoured him with his patronage, benefiting the gardens as much as he could, by adding to the collection. Mr. Atkins chose this site for his gardens, believing it to be far enough out of town for the convenience of the public, and healthy enough for the due growth of his trees and plants, and the well-being of his animals. The Zoological Gardens were, under Mr. Atkin's management, very different, by all accounts, from what they are now. I have seen on fine summer days, numbers of ladies of the highest respectability taking the air in them, accompanied by their children, while at night the attendance was most excellent, being patronized by the highest families in the town who seemed to enjoy the amusements provided with the utmost zest and relish. The collection of animals was remarkable at that time. Captains of vessels frequently brought rare and curious animals as presents, so that every week some new specimen of interest was added. I look back with pleasure to the many hours I have spent in the Gardens shortly after their being opened. They were admirably conducted, and in great repute as a zoological collection. Mr. Atkins took his idea of forming them from the success of the Gardens then lately established in Regent's Park, and at Kennington, in Surrey.

A great sensation was once produced by the abduction of a Miss Turner from Miss Daulby's School, on the West Derby-road, by Mr. E. Gibbon Wakefield. This is the white house that stands retired a field distant from the road, on the right hand side, about a quarter of a mile beyond the Zoological Gardens.

The abduction took place in March, 1826. It caused immense excitement throughout England. Miss Turner was the daughter of Mr. Turner, of Shrigley Park, Cheshire. By means of a forged letter addressed to Miss Daulby, intimating that Miss Turner's mother was dangerously ill, the young lady was permitted to leave the school for the purpose of going home. In the carriage in waiting was Mr. E. Gibbon Wakefield, a widower with one child (a perfect stranger to Miss Turner). It is believed he had been put up to this disgraceful act of villainy by a Miss Davies, with whom he was acquainted in Paris, and who was a member of a small coterie of friends, meeting for social purposes at each other's houses. This Miss Davies afterwards became the wife of Mr. E. G. Wakefield's father. She was tried with her two stepsons for the conspiracy. The object in taking Miss Turner away was the large fortune in expectancy from her father as his sole child and heiress. Miss Turner was taken from Liverpool to Manchester, next to Kendal, and on to Carlisle, and thence across the borders and there married to Mr. Wakefield; he having represented to her that by marrying him, he could save her father from impending ruin. From Scotland, they went to London, thence to Calais, where Miss Turner was found by her relatives and taken away.

The Wakefields were tried at Lancaster. Edward was found guilty of abduction and sentenced to transportation. He went to Australia in pursuance of his sentence, and after some years became the Government commissioner. The marriage with Miss Turner was not consummated. Miss Turner stated that she had received the utmost politeness and attention from Mr. Wakefield, and had been treated by him with deference and respect throughout. Had it not been for Mr. Wakefield's forbearance, it was thought that his sentence would have been different. Edward Gibbon Wakefield was said to have been a natural son of Lord Sandwich. He wrote some exceedingly clever works upon colonial matters, and on emigration.

# CHAPTER IX.

In the fields at the top of Brownlow-hill lane, just where Clarence and Russell-streets now meet, there was once a Powder House, to which vessels used to send their gunpowder while in port. This Powder House, in the middle of the last century, was a source of anxiety to the inhabitants of the town, who fully anticipated, at any moment, a blow-up, and the destruction of the town. The Powder House was afterwards converted into a receptacle for French prisoners. My grandfather knew the place well.

It does not require a man to be very old to remember the pleasant appearance of Moss Lake Fields, with the Moss Lake Brook, or Gutter, as it was called, flowing in their midst. The fields extended from Myrtle-street to Paddington, and from the top of Mount Pleasant or Martindale's-hill, to the rise at Edge-hill. The brook ran parallel with the present Grove-street, rising somewhere about Myrtle-street. In olden times, before coal was in general use, Moss Lake Fields were used as a "Turbary," a word derived from the French word *Tourbiere*, a turf field. (From the way that the turf is dried we have our term *topsy turvy, i.e.,* top side turf way). Sir Edward More, in his celebrated rental, gives advice to his son to look after "his turbary." The privilege of turbary, or "getting turf," was a valuable one, and was conferred frequently on the burgesses of towns paying scot and lot. I believe turf, fit for burning, has been obtained from Moss Lake Fields even recently. Just where Oxford-street is now intersected by Grove-street, the brook opened out into a large pond, which was divided into two by a bridge and road communicating between the meadows on each side. The bridge was of stone of about four feet span, and rose above the meadow level. The sides of the approach were protected by wooden railings, and a low parapet went across the bridge. [167] Over the stone bridge the road was carried when connection was opened to Edge-hill from Mount Pleasant, and Oxford-street was laid out. When the road was planned both sides of it were open fields and pastures. The first Botanic Gardens were laid out in this vicinity; they extended to Myrtle-street, the entrance Lodge stood nearly on the site of the Deaf and Dumb Asylum. In winter the Moss Lake Brook usually overflowed and caused a complete inundation. On this being frozen over fine skating was enjoyed for a considerable space. The corporation boundary line was at this side of the brook. In summer the volunteers sometimes held reviews upon these fields, when all the beauty and fashion of the town turned out to witness the sight. At this time all the land at the top of Edge-hill was an open space called the Greenfields, on part of which Edge-hill church is built. Mason-street was merely an occupation lane. The view from the rising ground, at the top of Edge-hill, was very fine, overlooking the town and having the river and the Cheshire shore in the background. Just where Wavertree-lane, as it was called, commences there was once a large reservoir, which extended for some distance towards the Moss Lake Fields, Brownlow-hill Lane being carried over it.

While we are wandering in this neighbourhood there must not be forgotten a word or two about Mr. Joseph Williamson (who died about 1841) and his excavations at Edge-hill. As I believe there is no authentic record of him, or of them, so far as I can recollect, a brief description of him and his strange works may not be uninteresting to the old, who have heard both spoken of, and to the present generation who know nothing of their extent and his singularity. It certainly does appear remarkable, but it is a fact, that many people possess a natural taste for prosecuting underground works. There is so much of mystery, awe, and romance in anything subterranean, that we feel a singular pleasure in instituting and making discoveries in it, and it is not less strange than true that those who once begin making excavations seem loth to leave off. Mr. Williamson appears to have been a true Troglodite, one who preferred the Cimmerian darkness of his vaulted world, to the broad cheerful light of day. He spent the principal part of his time in his vaults and excavations, and literally lived in a cellar, for his sitting room was little else, being a long vault with a window at one end, and his bedroom was a cave hollowed out at the back of it. In his cellar it was that he dispensed his hospitalities, in no sparing manner, having usually casks of port and sherry on tap, and also a cask of London porter. Glasses were out of use with him. In mugs and jugs were the generous fluids drawn and drank. When Williamson made a man welcome that welcome was sincere. Before I say anything about the excavations, a few "Recollections" of Joseph himself are worthy to be recorded. He was born on the 10th of March, 1769, at Warrington, and commenced his career in Liverpool, with Mr. Tate the tobacco merchant, in Wolstenholme-square. Williamson used to tell his own tale by stating that "I came to Liverpool a poor lad to make my fortune. My mother was a decent woman, but my father was the greatest rip that ever walked on two feet. The poor woman took care that all my clothes were in good order, and she would not let me come to Liverpool unless I lodged with my employer. I got on in the world little by little, until I became a man of substance, and I married Betty Tate, my master's daughter. When the wedding day arrived I told her I would meet her at the (St. Thomas') church, which I did, and after it was all over I mounted the horse which was waiting for me, and told Betty to go home and that I would come to her after the Hunt. I was a member of the then famous 'Liverpool Hunt,' and when I got to the Meet somebody said, 'Why, Williamson, how smart you are!'—'Smart,' said I, 'aye!—a man should look smart on his wedding day!' 'Wedding day,' exclaimed some of the fellows, 'Who have you married?' 'I haven't married anybody,' I said, 'but the parson has married me to old Tate's daughter!' 'Why, where's your wife?' 'She's at home, to be sure, where all good wives ought to be—getting ready her husband's dinner.' I'll tell you what, Betty and I lived but a cat and dog life of it, but I was sorry to part with the old girl when she did go." On the day of Mrs. Williamson's funeral, the men employed on the works were seen lounging about doing nothing. Williamson noticed this, and inquired the reason? They told him that it was out of respect for their mistress. "Oh! stuff," said Williamson, "you work for the living, not for the dead. If you chaps don't turn to directly, I shall stop a day's wages on Saturday."

Mr. Williamson's appearance was remarkable. His hat was what might have been truly called "a shocking bad one." He generally wore an old and very much patched brown coat, corduroy breeches, and thick, slovenly shoes; but his underclothing was always of the finest description, and faultless in cleanliness and colour. His manners were ordinarily rough and uncouth, speaking gruffly, bawling loudly, and even rudely when he did not take to any one. Yet, strange to say, at a private dinner or evening party, Mr. Williamson exhibited a gentleness of manner, when he chose, which made him a welcome guest. His fine, well-shaped, muscular figure fully six feet high, his handsome head and face made him, when well-dressed, present a really distinguished appearance. He seemed to be possessed of two opposite natures—the rough and the smooth. It was said that once, on a Royal Duke visiting Liverpool, he received a salute from Williamson, and was so struck with its gracefulness that he inquired who he was, and remarked that "it was the most courtly bow he had seen out of St. James's." Williamson was very fond of children. The voice of a little one could at any time soothe him when irritable. He used to say of them, "Ah, there's no deceit in children. If I had had some, I should not have been the *arch*-rogue I am.". The industrious poor of Edge-hill found in Williamson a ready friend in time of need, and when work was slack many a man has come to the pay-place on Saturday, who had done nothing all the week but dig a hole and fill it up again. Once, on being remonstrated with by a man he had thus employed, on the uselessness of the work, Williamson said, "You do as you are told—you honestly earn the money by the sweat of your brow, and the mistress can go to market on Saturday night—I don't want you to think."

He often regaled his work-people with a barrel of ale or porter, saying they "worked all the better for their throats being wetted." His vast excavations when they were in their prime, so to speak, must have been proof of the great numbers of men he employed. He always said that he never made a penny by the sale of the stone. He gave sufficient, I believe, to build St. Jude's Church. He used vast quantities on his own strange structures.

A lady of my acquaintance once caught Williamson intently reading a book. She inquired its purport. He evaded the question, but being pressed, told her it was the Bible, and expressed a wish that he had read much more of it, and studied it, and that he always found something new in it every time he opened it. This lady said that the touching way, the graceful expression of Mr. Williamson's manner, when he said this, took her completely by surprise, having been only accustomed to his roughness and ruggedness. He added, "The Bible tells me what a rascal I am." Mr. Stephenson, the great engineer, inspected the excavations, and it was with pride Mr. Williamson repeated Mr. Stephenson's expressions of high estimation of his works. Mr. Stephenson said they were the most astonishing works he had ever seen in their way. When the tunnel to Lime-street from Edge-hill was in progress, one day, the excavators were astonished to find the earth giving way under them, and to see men actually under the tunnel they were then forming. On encountering Mr. Williamson, he told them "he could show them how to tunnel if they wanted to learn a lesson in that branch of art." It seemed a strange anomaly, and quite unaccountable that Mr. Williamson should be so chary in allowing any strangers to visit his excavations. He seemed to keep them for his own gratification, and it was with the greatest difficulty permission could be obtained to go through them. He would say to the numberless persons who applied, "they were not show-shops, nor he a showman." When he did grant permission he always gave the obliged parties fully and unmistakably to understand that he was conferring upon them a great favour. His temper was suspicious. I recollect being told of a person calling on him, to pay a long over-due rent account for another person, when, as Williamson was handing over the receipt, and about to take up the money, he suddenly fixed his keen eye upon his visitor, and asked him what trick he was going to play him, as it seemed strange that he should pay money for another man. "Take your money away, sir," said he, "and come again to-morrow; there is something underhand in your proceedings, and I'll not be done." For some of his tenants he used to execute cheerfully the most costly alterations, while for others he would not expend a shilling, and would let his premises go to rack, rather than put in a nail for them.

There was a house of his once standing at the corner of Bolton-street, which he built entirely for a whim. It was a great square house, with enormously wide and long windows. It was of three stories, two upper tiers and a basement. There was no kitchen to it, no conveniences of any kind sufficient to render it habitable. From the cellar there was a tunnel which ran under Mason-street to the vaults opposite. He built it intending it for his friend, Mr. C. H---, the artist, who had one day complained of the bad light he had to paint in, and Mr. Williamson told him he would remedy that evil if he would wait a bit. Presently he commenced the house in Bolton-street, and when it was completed the artist was sent for, and told that it had been built for him as a studio. Mr. H--- stood aghast on seeing the immense windows, and could not make Mr. Williamson understand that an artist's light was not wanted in quantity but quality. Williamson swore lustily at H---'s obstinacy, and could not be made to understand what was really required. A reverend gentleman, still living and highly respected, who happened to be passing along the street, was called in to give his opinion on the subject by Mr. W. He, however, joined issue with Mr. H---, but neither could make Mr. W. understand the matter. The rooms were very lofty and spacious, and if I recollect rightly each floor consisted of only one room. I believe it was never occupied. In High-street, Edge-hill, Mr. Williamson also built some houses which were skirted by Back Mason-street. The houses at the corner of High-street and Back Mason-street were built up from a quarry. They are as deep in cellarage as they are high, while the rooms in them are innumerable. Williamson used to call himself "King of Edge-hill," and had great influence over the work people residing in the neighbourhood. I knew a lady who once had an encounter with Williamson wherein she came off victorious, and carried successfully her point. The affair is curious. This lady, about 1838 or '39, wanted a house, and was recommended to go up to Edge-hill and endeavour to meet with Mr. Williamson and try to get on the right side of him, which was considered a difficult thing to do. She was told that he had always some large houses to let, and if she pleased him he would be a good landlord. Mrs. C---, accompanied by a lady, went up to Edge-hill and looked about as they were told to do for a handsome-looking man in a shabby suit of clothes. They were told that they were sure to find Mr. W. where men were working, as he always had some in his employ in one way or another in the neighbourhood. On arriving at Mason-street, sure enough, they espied the object of their search watching the operations of some bricklayers busily engaged in erecting the very house in Bolton-street just spoken of. Mrs. C---, who was a sharp, shrewd person, good looking and pleasant in her manners, sauntered up to Williamson and inquired of him if he knew of any houses to be let at Edge-hill. "Houses!" replied Williamson in his roughest and rudest style: "What should I know of houses, a poor working man like me!" "Well," said the lady, "I thought you might have known of some to let, and you need not be so saucy and ill-tempered." Williamson roughly rejoined, and the lady replied, and thus they got to a complete wordy contest attracting the attention of the bystanders, who were highly amused to find that Williamson had met his match. The lady's sarcasms and gibes seemed to make Williamson doubly crusty. He at length asked the other lady—who, by the way, was becoming nervous and half-frightened at what was going on—"what this woman," pointing to Mrs. C---, "would give for a house if she could meet with one to her mind." Mrs. C--- told him £30 per annum. Williamson burst out with an insulting laugh, and called all the men down from the house they were erecting, and when they had clustered round him he told them that "this woman wanted a house with ten rooms in it for £30 a year! Did they ever know of such an unreasonable request?" Of course the men agreed with their employer, and they were all dismissed after being regaled with a mug of porter each. Mrs. C--- narrowly watched Williamson and saw through him at once, and was not surprised on being invited to step into a house close by and see how she liked it. She found fault with some portions of the house and approved others. Williamson at length, after a short silence, inquired whether she really did want a house and would live in Mason-street. Mrs. C--- replied that she did really require one and liked the street very much. Williamson then asked her if she was in a hurry. On being told she was not, he bade her return that day fortnight at the same hour and he would try then to show her a house he thought would suit her exactly. With this the ladies departed, Williamson saying:—"There now, you be off; you come when I tell you; you'll find me a regular old screw; and if you don't pay your rent the day it is due I shall law you for it, so be off." Mrs. C--- then said, "My husband is a cockney, and I will bring him with me, and we will see if we can't turn the screw the right way." The ladies had no sooner arrived at the end of Mason-street, when on turning to take a last look of their singular friend they saw the men from the house in Bolton-street all following Williamson into the house they had just left, and as it eventually proved he had set them there and then to work to make the alterations she had suggested and desired.

On the termination of the fortnight the ladies called on their remarkable friend, and found him in waiting at the house with two great jugs of sherry and some biscuits on a table. He then took them over the house, and to their surprise found everything in it altered: two rooms had been opened into one, one room made into two, two had been made into three, and so on, and he asked Mrs. C--- if she was satisfied and if the house would suit her? He appeared to have completely gutted the house and reconstructed it. Putting it down at an unusually low rent for what had been done, the bargain was struck between the parties, and the landlord and his tenant were ever after good friends. He told the lady he liked her for sticking up to him "so manfully" and "giving him as good as he sent." Mr. Williamson took great delight in this lady's children and made great pets of them. On her family increasing the lady and her husband frequently asked Williamson to build her an extra room for a nursery, reminding him that as he was always building something, he might as well build them an extra room as anything else. He, however, declined until one day the lady sent him a manifesto from the "Queen Of Edge-hill," as he had been accustomed to call her, commanding him to build the room she wanted. Williamson, thereupon, wrote her a reply in the same strain, promising to attend to her commands.

A few mornings after his reply had been received the lady was busy in her bedroom dressing her baby, when she suddenly heard a loud knocking in the house adjoining, and down fell the wall, and amid the falling of bricks and the rising of dust Mr. Williamson himself appeared, accompanied by two joiners, who fitted a door into the opening, while two bricklayers quickly plastered up the walls. Through the door next stepped the landlord. "There, madam, what do you think of this room for a nursery," he exclaimed, "it is big enough if you had twenty children." Mr. Williamson had actually appropriated the drawing-room in his own house to her use. She thanked him, but said he might have given her some warning of what he was going to do, instead of covering her and the baby with dust, but Williamson laughed heartily at his joke, while the lady was glad to get a noble room added to her house without extra rent. This lady told me that one night just previous to this event they had heard a most extraordinary rumbling noise in Mr. Williamson's house which continued for a long time and it appeared to proceed from one of the lower rooms. On inquiring next day of Mr. Williamson what was the cause of the disturbance he took the lady into a large dining-room, where she found about fifty newly-painted blue barrows with red wheels all ranged along the room in rows. These had been constructed for the use of his labourers and were there stored away until wanted.

My acquaintance told me that one night they heard in the vaults below their house the most frightful shrieks and screams, and the strangest of noises, but they never could ascertain what was the cause of the commotion. The noises seemed to proceed from directly below their feet, and yet they fancied they came from some distance. The cries were not those of a person in agony, but a strange mixture of most unaccountable sounds.

A good story is told of a quaint speech made to Williamson by the Rev. Dr. Raffles. The Doctor and the Rev. Mr. Hull, who were neighbours, and, I fancy, tenants of Williamson's, were once met by him walking together, when W. exclaimed "I say, if I'd my way you two should be made bishops."

Dr. Raffles very quickly replied, "Ah, Williamson, you ought to be an *arch*bishop!" alluding to his well-known predilection for vault building. He once invited a party of gentlemen to dine with him. The guests were shown into a bare room with a deal table on trestles in the middle, with common forms on each side. Williamson, with the utmost gravity, bade his friends take their seats, placing himself at the head of the table. Facing each of the guests was a plate of porridge and some hard biscuits of which they were invited to partake. Some of the party taking this as an insulting joke, rose and left the room. Williamson, with the utmost grace, bowed them out without explanation. When the seceders had retired, a pair of folding doors were thrown open, exhibiting a large room with a costly feast prepared, to which the remainder of the party adjourned, laughing heartily over the trick that had been played and the agreeable surprise in store for them. Another good story is told of Mr. Williamson. He possessed some property at Carlisle which gave him a vote at the elections. Sir James Graham's committee sent him a circular, as from Sir James, soliciting his vote and interest. On receipt of this letter Williamson flew into a violent passion, went down to Dale-street there and then, took a place in the North Mail, proceeded to Carlisle, obtained one of Sir James Graham's placards from the walls, and posted back to Liverpool without delay. On his arrival at home he enclosed the obnoxious circular and placard in a parcel which he addressed with a most abusive letter to Sir James Graham, in which he charged him with such a string of political crimes as must have astonished the knight of Netherby, winding up the abuse by asking how he dared to solicit an honest man for his vote and by what right he had taken so unwarrantable a liberty.

# CHAPTER X.

In the last chapter of my "Recollections" I spoke of the man—Joseph Williamson; the present will be of his "excavations." In various parts of the world we find, on and under the surface, divers works of human hands that excite the wonder of the ignorant, the notice of the intelligent, and the speculation of the learned. Things are presented to our view, in a variety of forms, which must have been the result of great labour and cost, and which appear utterly useless and inapplicable to any ostensibly known purpose. Respecting many of these mysterious records of a past age, page after page has been written to prove, and even disprove, the supposed intent of their constructors; and it cannot but be admitted that after perusing many an erudite disquisition, we are sometimes as well-informed, and as near arriving at a conclusion as to the original purpose for which the object under discussion was intended, as when our attention was first engaged in it. In some instances, those who have discovered uses for the strange remnants of, to us, a dark age, have exceeded in ingenuity the projectors of those relics.

Could we draw aside the thick veil that hides the future from us, we might perhaps behold our great seaport swelling into a metropolis, in size and importance, its suburbs creeping out to an undreamt-of distance from its centre; or we might, reversing the picture, behold Liverpool by some unthought-of calamity—some fatal, unforeseen mischance, some concatenation of calamities—dwindled down to its former insignificance: its docks shipless, its warehouses in ruins, its streets moss-grown, and in its decay like some bye-gone cities of the east, that once sent out their vessels laden with "cloth of blue, and red barbaric gold." Under which of these two fates will Liverpool find its lot some centuries hence?—which of these two pictures will it then present? Be it one or the other, the strange undertakings of Joseph Williamson will perhaps, some centuries from now, be brought again to light, and excite as much marvel and inquiry as any mysterious building of old, the purpose of which we do not understand, and the use of which we cannot now account for. They will be seemingly as meaningless as any lonely cairn, isolated broken piece of wall, or solitary fragment of a building, of which no principal part remains, and which puzzles us to account for at the present time.

Mr. Williamson's property at Edge-hill, was principally held under the Waste Lands Commission. His leases expired in 1858. It commenced adjoining Miss Mason's house, near Paddington, and extended to Grinfield-street. It was bounded on the west by Smithdown-lane, along which ran a massive stone wall of singular appearance, more like that of a fortress than a mere enclosure. Within this area were some of the most extraordinary works, involving as great an outlay of money as may be found anywhere upon the face of the earth, considering the space of ground they occupy. In their newly-wrought state, about the years 1835 and '36, or thereabouts, they created intense wonder in the minds of the very few who were permitted to examine them. During the last few years, I believe they have been gradually filled up and very much altered, but they are still there to be laid open some day. Few of us know much of them, though so few years have elapsed since they were projected and carried out, since the sounds of the blast, the pick, and the shovel were last heard in their vicinity. Now what will be said of these minings, subterranean galleries, vaults and arches, should they suddenly be discovered a century hence, when their originator as well as their origin shall have faded away into nothing like the vanishing point of the painter? Here we behold an astonishing instance of the application of vast labour without use, immense expense incurred without hope of return, and, if we except the asserted reason of the late projector that these works were carried on for the sole purpose of employing men in times of great need and depression, we have here stupendous works without perceptible motive, reason, or form. Like the catacombs at Paris, Williamson's vaults might have been made receptacles for the dried bones of legions of our forefathers. Again, they might have been converted into fitting places for the hiding of stolen goods, or where the illicit distiller might carry on his trade with impunity.

I hardly know in what tense to speak of those excavations, not being aware in what state they are at present. A strange place it is, or was. Vaulted passages cut out of the solid rock; arches thrown up by craftmen's hands, beautiful in proportion and elegant in form, but supporting nothing. Tunnels formed here—deep pits there. Yawning gulfs, where the fetid, stagnant waters threw up their baneful odours. Here the work is finished off, as if the mason had laboured with consummate skill to complete his work, so that all the world might see and admire, although no human eyes, save those of the master's, would ever be set upon it. Here lies the ponderous stone as it fell after the upheaving blast had dislodged it from its bed; and there, vaulted over, is a gulf that makes the brain dizzy, and strikes us with terror as we look down into it. Now we see an arch, fit to bridge a mountain torrent; and in another step or two we meet another, only fit to span a simple brook.

Tiers of passages are met with, as dangerous to enter as they are strange to look at. It must ever be a matter of regret that after Mr. Williamson's death, some one able to make an accurate survey of the property did not go through and describe it, because it has been greatly changed since then by the accumulations of rubbish that have been brought to every part of it. All the most elaborate portions of the excavations have been entirely closed up. In one section of the ground (that near Grinfield-street), where there was of late years a joiner's shop, the ground was completely undermined in galleries and passages, one over the other, constituting a subterranean labyrinth of the most intricate design. Near here also was a deep gulf, in the wall sides of which were two houses completely excavated out of the solid rock, each having four rooms of tolerable dimensions.

This chasm is now quite filled up. The terrace extending from Grinfield-street to Miss Mason's house is threaded with passages, vaults, and excavations. At the northern corner there is a tunnel eight feet high, and as many wide, which runs up from what was once an orchard and garden, to a house in Mason-street. The tunnel is, I should think, 60 yards long. As the ground rises up the hill, there are several flights of stone steps with level resting-places. About two-thirds up, where the first flight is encountered, may be seen a portion of a large vault which runs a short way southwardly. A small portion of the top of the arch, between it and the steps, is left open, but for what reason I never could make out. The further end of this vault opens into another great vault, which I shall presently describe. The passage is very dry, but the air has a cold "gravey" taint, very unpleasant to inhale. At the second landing there is a sort of recess, into which rubbish from the garden above is shot down through a spout or funnel. At the top of the passage is a doorway opening upon the back of a house in Mason-street. This passage or tunnel was evidently intended for a mode of communication between the house and the orchard. In the garden or orchard, and near the tunnel mouth, were four lofty recesses, like alcoves, three of which were four feet deep. In one of those recesses, which was carried much further back than the others, the stones were lying as they fell, and there was a channel on one side of the flooring which seemed to have been intended for a drain. Through a large folding gate access is obtained from Smithdown-lane into a wide passage or vault, in shape like a seaman's speaking trumpet. It is broad enough to accommodate two carts at least, and has been used when the stone has been carted away from the delph at its eastern end. This vault is constructed of brick. It gradually deepens at the eastern end, and is about 15 feet wide, and 20 high. At the opening it is not more than 15 high. The top outside is covered by soil, and forms part of the garden previously mentioned. At the left hand side of the tunnel end will be found a vault, running northward for about fifty or sixty feet. The end of this vault is the limit of Mr. Williamson's property. The tunnel already described as running up to Mason-street crosses the top of this vault. This vault is about thirty-six feet wide and perhaps thirty feet high, but the floor has been considerably raised since Mr. Williamson's time by debris and rubbish of all sorts thrown into it. In the right hand corner of the vault, about ten feet from the ground, there is the mouth of a tunnel which runs up first towards Mason-street, it then turns and winds in a variety of ways in passages continuing under the houses in Mason-street, and opening upon many of the vaults. To the left of the entrance vault, there is a large square area from which immense masses of red sandstone have been quarried. It is forty feet from side to side. There is a vault in the southern wall opposite the wall just described. It runs towards Grinfield-street, and is composed of two large arches side by side, surmounted by two smaller ones. In the eastern face of the quarry there is an immense arch perhaps sixty feet high; and about thirty feet from its entrance there is an immense and massive stone pier from which spring two arches on each side, one above the other, but not from the same level. The pier is hollowed on the inside by three arches. On the left hand wall inside the arch there are two large arches, from which vaults run northwardly, and on the right hand side of the wall there are also two vaults which extend to a great distance in a southwardly direction, towards Grinfield-street. From these vaults, other vaults branch off in all sorts of directions. The houses in Mason-street all rest upon these arches; and as you passed along the street, the depth of some of them at one time was visible through the grids. The construction of these arches is of the most solid description, and seems stable as the earth itself. There are some openings of vaults commenced at the end near Grinfield-Street, but discontinued. These arches seem to have given way and presented a curiously ruined aspect. In the lower range of vaults there was a run of water and what Williamson called "a quagmire." In several places there are deep wells, whence the houses in Mason-Street seem to be supplied with water. Sections of arches commenced, but left unfinished, were visible at one time in various places. The lowest range of arches opening from the Grinfield-street end run to the northward. From the roof of many of these vaults were stalactites, but of no great length. The terraced gardens are ranged on arches all solidly built. The houses in Mason-street are strange constructions. In one house I saw there was no window in one good-sized room, light being obtained through a funnel carried up to the roof of the house through an upper floor and room. This strange arrangement arose from Mr. Williamson having no plan of the house he was building for the men to work by, consequently it was found the windows had been forgotten. He never had, I believe, any drawings or plans of either his houses or excavations. The men were told to work on till he ordered them to stop. In another house I went through there was an immense room which appeared as if two stories had been made into one. The bedroom—I believe there was only one in the house—was gained by an open staircase, run up by the side of the west wall of the large room. After passing the room door you mounted another flight of stairs which terminated in a long lobby, which ran over the top of the adjoining house, to two attics. The gardens of this house were approached by going down several stone steps (all was solid with Mr. Williamson) past the kitchen, which was also arched, and thence down another flight of stone steps until you came to a lofty vaulted passage of great breadth. You then entered a dry, wide arch. From this another arch opened in a northwardly direction. At the end of the principal vault was a long, narrow, vaulted passage, which was lighted by a long iron grating which proved to be a walk in a garden belonging to two houses at a distance. This passage then shot off at right angles, and at length a garden was gained on a terrace, the parapet wall of which overlooked the large opening or quarry previously described; and a fearful depth it appeared.

Some of the backs of the Mason-street houses project, some recede, some have no windows visible, others have windows of such length and breadth as must have thrown any feeble-minded tax-gatherer when he had to receive window duty into fits. These houses really appear as if built by chance, or by a blind man who has felt his way and been satisfied with the security of his dwelling rather than its appearance. The interiors of these houses, however, were very commodious, when I saw them years ago. They were strangely arranged, with very large rooms and very small ones, and long passages oddly running about.

I recollect once going over a house in High-street which Williamson erected. The coal vault I went into would have held at least two hundred tons of coals. In all these vaults and places the rats swarmed in droves, and of a most remarkable size. I once saw one perfectly white. Wherever Williamson possessed property there did his "vaulting ambition" exhibit itself.

Such is a brief account of Williamson and his works. A book might be filled with his sayings and doings. Amid all his roughness he was a kind and considerate man, and did a great deal of good in his own strange way. His effects were sold by Trotter and Hodgkins on the 7th June, 1841, and one of the lots, No. 142, consisted of a view of Williamson's vaults and a small landscape. I wonder what has become of the former. Lot 171 was a "cavern scene" which showed the bent of the man's taste.

# CHAPTER XI.

The conversion of the huge stone quarry at the Mount into a cemetery was a very good idea. This immense excavation was becoming a matter of anxiety with the authorities, as to what should be done with so large an area of so peculiar a nature. To fill it up with rubbish seemed an impossibility; while the constant and increasing demand for stone added to the difficulties of the situation. The establishment of a cemetery at Kensal Green in Middlesex, suggested the conversion of this quarry to a similar purpose. A feeling in the minds of people that the dead should not be interred amidst the living, began to prevail—a feeling that has since grown so strong as to be fully recognised in the extensive cemeteries now formed at the outskirts of this and all large towns. Duke-street used to be called "The road to the Quarry," and was almost solely used by the carts bringing stone into the town. Eighty years ago, there were only a few houses at the top of this street, having gardens at the back. There was a ropery which extended from the corner of the present Berry-street (called after Captain Berry, who built the first house in it), to the roperies which occupied the site of the present Arcades. All above this was fields, with a few houses only in Wood-street, Fleet-street, Wolstenholme-square, and Hanover-street. This latter street contained some very handsome mansions, having large gardens connected with them.

Rodney-street was laid out by a German named Schlink, who, being desirous to perpetuate his name, called his new thoroughfare Schlink-street. Several houses were erected in it, but the idea of living in "Schlink"-street— the word "Schlink" being associated with bad meat—deterred persons from furthering the German's speculation. In deference to this notion, the name of the then popular hero, "Rodney," was given to the street; and it has continued to be occupied by families of the highest respectability, and especially of late years by the medical profession.

I recollect a rather curious circumstance, connected with one of the best houses in this street, which caused some amusement at the time amongst those who were acquainted with the particulars and the parties. It was a complete instance of "turning the tables." About thirty years, or more, ago, a gentleman lived in Rodney-street, whose commercial relations required him to be frequently in the metropolis. He found his presence there was likely to be continuous, and determined to give up his house in Liverpool and reside permanently in London. He, therefore, took steps to let his house (which he held under lease at one hundred and five pounds per annum) by advertising it, and putting a bill in the window to that effect. To his surprise he received a notice from his landlord informing him that by the tenure of his lease, to which he was referred, he would find that he could not sub-let. Finding this to be the case, he went to the owner of the property, and expressed a desire to be released from his occupancy on fair terms, offering to find a substantial tenant and pay half a year's rent. The landlord, knowing he had a good tenant, rejected this offer in a way somewhat approaching to rudeness. Finding himself tied to the stake, as it were, the gentleman inquired under what terms he could be released? The answer was, that nothing short of twelve months rent and a tenant, would suffice to obtain a release. Without making a reply to this proposal, the gentleman went his way. A few mornings after this interview, the owner of the house, in passing, saw a man painting the chequers [197] on the door cheeks, and on looking up found that "--- --- was licensed to sell beer by retail, to be drunk on the premises." Astonished at this proceeding, he ordered the painter to stop his work, but the painter told him he was paid for the job, and do it he would. On being told who it was that spoke to him his reply was that he did not care, and that he might go to a place "where beer is not sold by retail nor on the premises," for aught he cared. Furious at this insolence, the angry landlord sent word to his tenant that he wanted to see him, at the same time giving him notice of what he would do if he persisted in appropriating the house to the purpose intimated. The only answer returned was, that the tenant would be at "the beer-shop" at ten in the morning, where he would meet his landlord. At ten, accordingly, the old gentleman went to his tenant, and on meeting him asked him what was the meaning of his proceedings. "Why," replied the tenant, "I find by my lease that it is true I cannot sub-let, and as you will not accept what I consider fair terms of release, I intend, for the remainder of my term, to keep the place open as a beer-shop. I have taken out a license, bought furniture for the purpose, and here comes the first load of forms and tables" (at that moment, sure enough, up came a cart heavily laden with all sorts of beer-house requisites). "I intend to make the drawing-room a dancing saloon, and the garden a skittle alley. I have engaged an old warehouseman to manage the business for me, and if we don't do a roaring business, I hope to make enough to pay your rent, and become free from loss." The intense anger of the landlord may be imagined; and he left the house uttering threats of the utmost vengeance of the law; but on an interview with his attorney he found there was no redress—a beer-shop was "not in the bond." He, therefore, went again to his refractory tenant, for it was clear that if the house was once opened as a beer-shop, the adjoining property would be deteriorated. He was smilingly greeted, and his tenant regretted that he had not tapped his ale, or he would have offered him a glass. "Come, Mr. ---," said the landlord, "let us see if we cannot arrange this matter. I am now willing to accept your offer of half a year's rent, and a tenant." "No," said Mr. ---, "I cannot think of such terms now." "Well, then, suppose you give me a quarter's rent, and find me the tenant." "No!" "Then the rent without the tenant." "No!" "Then a tenant without the rent." "No; but I will tell you what I'll agree to, my good sir— you see, I have been put to some expense. I made you a fair, and, as I think, a liberal offer, which you would not accept. Now, if you will reimburse me all the expense I have been put to, and pay £10 to the town charities, I will abandon my beer-house scheme, undertake to give up the key, and close the account between us." With these terms the landlord eventually complied, thus having "the tables fairly turned" upon him.

Cock-fighting was at one time a favourite sport in Liverpool, amongst the lower orders, and, indeed, amongst all other classes too. In a street leading out of Pownall-square (so called after Mr. William Pownall, whose death was accelerated during his mayoralty in 1708, in consequence of a severe cold, caught in suppressing a serious riot of the Irish which occurred in the night-time in a place near the Salthouse Dock, called the Devil's acre), there was a famous cock-pit. The street is now called Cockspur-street. Where the cock-pit stood there is a small dissenting chapel, and the entrance to it may be found up a court. This cock-pit was the resort of all the low ruffians of the neighbourhood. In consequence of the disturbances which continually took place, it was suppressed as the neighbourhood increased in population. It is rather singular that in more than one instance cock-pits have been converted into places of public worship. The cock-pit at Aintree, for instance, was so converted; and the first sermon preached in it was by the Rev. Dr. Hume, who skilfully alluded to the scenes that had been enacted in it, without in the least offensively describing them. That sermon was a remarkable one, and made a great impression on the congregation assembled there for the first time. The late Lord Derby was an enthusiastic cock-fighter, and kept a complete set of trainers and attendants. When I was a boy, it was thought nothing of to attend a cock-fight, and, such was the passion for this cruel sport, that many lads used to keep cocks for the purpose.

It is a curious thing to watch the changes that have taken place from time to time in different neighbourhoods as to the character of the inhabitants. Where at one time we may have found the aristocracy of the town assembling, we have noticed its respectability gradually fading away, and those who inhabited large mansions removing elsewhere. For instance,

Rose-hill, Cazneau-street (called after Mr. Cazneau; at one time a pretty street indeed, with gardens in front of all the houses), and Beau-street, were fashionable suburban localities. St. Anne-street abounded in handsome mansions and was considered the court-end of the town. The courtly tide then set southward; Abercromby-square, and its neighbourhood sprung up, and so surged outward to Aigburth one way and to West Derby another. Everton I have already spoken of. I remember the houses in Faulkner-terrace remaining for years unfinished, and it was at one time called "Faulkner's Folly," from the notion that no one would ever think of living so far out of the town. Mr. Faulkner, however, proved himself to be more long-sighted than those who ridiculed his undertaking.

I remember the present Haymarket a field with a rivulet flowing through the midst of it, and the whole of this neighbourhood fields and gardens. In Cazneau-street there was an archery lodge, a portion of which is still standing.

I remember, too, the erection of Richmond Fair, in 1787. It was projected by a Mr. Dobb, who dwelt in a bay-windowed house still standing in St. Anne-street. He intended it for a Cloth Hall for the Irish factors to sell their linens in, which they brought in great quantities at that time to Liverpool. The Linen Hall at Chester gave him the idea of this undertaking. It took very well at first, but in consequence of complaints being made by the shopkeepers in the town that the dealers in linen, instead of selling wholesale were carrying on an extensive retail trade and injuring their business, the authorities stopped all further traffic in it, and, after remaining some years unoccupied, it has of late been converted into small tenements.

# CHAPTER XII.

Thirty years ago Great Charlotte-street, at the Ranelagh-street end, was a narrow, poorly-built thoroughfare. On the left hand side, looking south, between Elliot-street and the present coach-builders' establishment, there was a timber-yard, in which stood a small wooden theatre, known as "Holloway's *Sans Pareil*," and truly it was *Sans Pareil*, for surely there was nothing like it, either in this town or anywhere else. Both inside and outside it was dirty and dingy. There were only a pit and gallery, the latter taking the place of boxes in other theatres; and, yet the scenery was excellent, the actors, many of them, very clever, and the getting up of the pieces as good as could be in so small a place. The pantomimes at Christmas were capital. The charges of admission were: to the pit 3d., and to the gallery, 6d. The audiences, whether men or women, boys or girls, were the roughest of the rough. The quantity of copper coin taken at the doors was prodigious; and I am told that it occupied two persons several hours, daily, to put the money up into the usual five-shilling packages. Mr. Holloway used to stand at one door and his wife at the other, to receive the admission money. When the audience was assembled, the former would go into the pit and there pack the people, so that no space should be lost. He would stuff a boy into one, or a little girl into another seat, and leave them to settle down into their proper places; giving one a buffet and another a knock on the head, just to encourage the others to keep order and be obedient to his will and wish. There was no space lost in the pit of Holloway's theatre, whatever there might be anywhere else. A thriving business was carried on in this little bit of a theatre, and if the highest class of performances was not produced, nothing at any time offensive to order and morality was permitted.

I remember a good joke in which a gentlemen whom I knew, connected with one of our newspapers, and a leading actress at the Theatre Royal, were concerned, in connection with a visit to the *Sans Pareil*. The lady was very desirous to see a piece which was got up with great *eclat* at the *Sans Pareil*, and which was attracting crowds of people to see it. I think it was entitled "Maria Martin; or, the Murder at the Red Barn." Having expressed her wish to my friend, he at once offered to escort her any evening on which she was disengaged. Fixing, therefore a night when her services in Williamson-square were not required, my friend and the fair *comedienne* betook themselves to

Great Charlotte-street and presented themselves at the gallery door where the gentleman tendered the price of their admission. Now the lady had a thick veil on that she might, as she hoped, conceal her well-known features. But it seems that Mr. Holloway had at once recognised his fair visitor. On the money being tendered to Mrs. Holloway at the gallery door, Mr. H. called out from his door, "Pass 'em in—all right, missus." Now my friend was well aware that Mr. Holloway knew him, and therefore supposed that as a press man he would not allow him to pay—not supposing for a minute that the muffled up figure of his companion had been recognised.

So in they went and managed to climb up the half ladder, half stair, that led to the "aristocratic" region of the auditory part of the theatre. These stairs were frightfully dirty and steep. A broom had not been near them for months, and the lady, picking up her ample skirts, endeavoured to avoid all contact with both stairs and walls. On emerging from the top landing into the theatre, they found the place in a state of semi-darkness. They could just make out a few rows of benches, and clustering in the middle front were about thirty people. The noise was horrible, and seemed more so through the prevailing darkness. Shoutings, bawlings, whistlings, and screamings were in full swing, and the lady paused for a moment, whispering to her companion, "Oh, let's go back—I can't stand this at any price."

My friend, however, urged his companion to remain, and at length they managed to scramble forward, and secure a front seat at one side. The clamour was now added to by the entrance of the band, who mingled the sounds of tuning instruments with the other discords prevalent. Just at this juncture in came Mr. Holloway, who commenced the packing process, much to the amusement of our lady friend, who now began, in spite of the heat, the offensive smells, and the row, to become curious, and determined to see all that was to be seen. Presently the lights were fully turned on, and the orchestra struck up a lively medley tune, suitable to the taste of the audience. The orchestra, though small, was a good one, and some very clever performers were amongst its members. The play at length commenced, and appeared to create great interest and command attention. The lady admitted that the characters were well represented, and the drama very creditably got up. At length came a very sensational portion of the play. That part where *Maria Martin* is enticed into the Red Barn by *Corder*. In this exciting scene, *Maria*, as if having a presentiment of her fate, stands still and refuses to move. She appears in a state of stupor and *Corder* endeavours to urge her to accompany him. Now there were seated in the middle of the pit two sweeps, who appeared deeply interested in the performance, and finding that *Corder* could not induce *Maria* to go forward, one of them, amidst the silence that the cunning of the scene had commanded, screamed out—"Why don't you give her some snuff, and make her sneeze!" The silence thus broken was broken indeed, and the house roared with laughter. Our two friends were not backward in partaking of the merriment. The lady went almost into hysterics, so violent were her paroxysms of mirth. In the midst of the clamour, Holloway, hearing these loud bursts of laughter at a time when there should be complete silence, rushed on to the stage, fancying something had gone wrong. Darting to the footlights, as well as his little fat figure would let him, he roared out, "What's all this here row about?" and glancing round to see on whom he could heap his vengeance, he caught sight of our two friends, and looking up indignantly at them, he continued—"I von't have no row in my the-a-ter. If you vants to kick up a row you'd better go the The-a-ter R'yal." The audience seeing Mr. Holloway addressing the gallery, all eyes were now turned up to where our friends were seated, and the lady, (who had thrown up her veil in consequence of the intense heat) being recognised, was saluted by some one shouting out "Three cheers for Mrs. ---," whereupon the audience began hurrahing, in the midst of which our two adventurers made off as quickly as they could. They declared that neither of them could tell how they did so, being conscious of nothing until they found themselves breathing the fresh air in Lime-street.

When Stephen Price, the American manager, was in Liverpool beating up recruits, in, I think, 1831, Templeton, the tenor singer, was playing at the Theatre Royal. At that time Madame Malibran had made Templeton famous, by selecting him to enact the part of *Elvino* to her *Amina*, and thus a very second-rate singer suddenly jumped into the first place in public opinion, by his association with the gifted woman who enchanted all her hearers. Templeton waited on Price relative to an engagement in America, when the following conversation took place:—"I should like to go to America, Mr. Price, if you and I could agree about terms." "Very good, Mr. Templeton. What would you expect, Mr. Templeton?" "Well, I should just expect my passage out and home, and thirty 'punds' a week, Mr. Price, to begin with." "Very good, Mr. Templeton." "And all my travelling expenses, from toun to toun." "Very good, Mr. Templeton. Anything else, Mr. Templeton?" "My board and lodging in every toun, Mr. Price." "Very good, Mr. Templeton. Any thing else, Mr. Templeton?" "And a clear benefit in every toun, also, Mr. Price." "Very good. Anything else, Mr. Templeton?" "Well—no—I—ah—no!—nothing occurs to me just now, Mr. Price." "Well, then," said Mr. Price, "I'll see you d---d first, Mr. Templeton."

There was a very good story current in Liverpool, some twenty-five years ago, about Mr. W. J. Hammond, a then great favourite, both as actor and manager, and an acquaintance of mine. About that time a very flashy gentleman went into the Adelphi Hotel, and after making minute inquiry as to the bill of fare, and what he could have for dinner, at length ordered "a mutton chop to be ready for him at five o'clock." Five o'clock came, and also the traveller, who sat down in the coffee room to his banquet. He helped himself to the water at his own table and then emptied the bottles at the next, and at length called on the waiter for a further supply. When the mutton chop was duly finished, the waiter inquired what wine his "lordship" would take. "Oh!—ah!—wine! I'll take—another bottle of—'water.'" "Pray, sir," said the waiter (leaning the tips of his thumbs upon the table) with a most insinuating manner—"Pray, sir, would you like the *Bootle* or the *Harrington* water?" Hammond heard this, and agreed, with the friend referred to, to enter the Hotel, one at each door, and severally call out, one for a glass of "Harrington," and the other for a glass of "Bootle" water. "Waiter, some Bootle water!" came from a voice at the Copperas-hill door. "Waiter, some Harrington water!" was the order proceeding from the traveller entering by the front door. These strange orders, breaking upon the stillness that pervades this well-conducted hotel, seemed to excite great surprise in one or two aristocratic guests, who were standing in the lobby, when just at the moment Mr. Radley came out of one of the rooms and recognised the jokers. Taking them into his sanctum, he provided them with something stronger than the stream from the good old red sandstone. After a short time Mr. R. was called out, and the two guests began to get impatient at his non-return. Hammond declared that he must go—so did his friend; but they both thought it would seem unmannerly to leave the hotel without seeing their entertainer. Which should remain? However, Hammond soon cut the matter short by bolting out of the room and locking the door. His friend sat patiently enough for some little time, fully expecting Mr. Radley's return, but, while waiting, fell asleep. When he awoke he found himself in darkness, wondering where he could possibly be. After groping about some time, he discovered that the door was locked. The trick Hammond had played him then flashed across his mind. Hunting about, he at length found the bell which soon brought some one to the door, and on its being opened a rather severe questioning took place, as to how the visitor got there and what was his object. Mr. Radley having in the meantime gone home, he could not be referred to. It was only after sending for some person who knew the gentleman that he was released, and certainly not without some suspicions attaching to his visit and his peculiar position.

I recollect a good anecdote of a favourite actor in Liverpool some twenty years ago, when he was engaged at the Theatre Royal as one of the stock company. Mr. S--- was a constant church-goer, as many actors and actresses are, although those who do not know them fancy they cannot be either good or religious—a great mistake. Mr. S--- was accommodated by a friend, who had a very handsomely fitted up pew in St. A---'s Church, with the use of it, and Mr. S--- occupied it so long that he quite considered it to be his own; and it was a standing joke amongst his intimates that on all occasions "my pew" was referred to. Being out one night rather late, with some "jolly companions," he and they found, on comparing timepieces, that if they were not quick in getting home unpleasant consequences would ensue amongst their domestic relations. Said one, "I must be off." Said another, "If I don't make haste shall be locked out." "My boy," said S---, "never mind being locked out, I'll go and get the key of St. A---'s church, and you shall *sleep in my pew!*"

# CHAPTER XIII.

On turning over my "Recollections" of our theatre, there was one circumstance connected with the drama in Liverpool that I shall not forget. It made a great impression on my mind, as it did no doubt upon all those who, at the time, interested themselves in the success of the movement. I allude to the brilliant demonstration that took place in December, 1816, when an amateur performance was got up in aid of the distress experienced in Liverpool, a distress felt in common with the whole nation. All the leading theatrical and musical amateurs in the town took part in that performance. I dare say that, at this distance of time even, it is well remembered by those who assisted at it, if there be any of them still amongst as. I am quite certain that the patriotic feelings which urged them to unite and give their valuable services at so trying a time must still and ever be a source of gratification to them of the highest order.

At the date I refer to, great commercial distress prevailed. Amongst the working and lower classes the most frightful indigence and destitution were experienced.

After the battle of Waterloo all sorts of property depreciated in value. Everything previously was at a "war price." The amount of taxation which the country had to endure may be judged when I state that for a house rented at forty pounds per annum the following were the taxes levied upon its occupier:—Window tax, £11 4s. 6d.; inhabited house duty, £2 18s. 6.; land tax, £1 16s.; highway and church rates, £2 13s. 9d.; poor rates, £18; making a total to be paid of £36 12s. 9d.! The failure of the harvest that year added also to the general distress so that the nation might have been said to have been on the very eve of bankruptcy. So bad was the flour in 1816, and so scanty the supply, that everybody seemed occupied in hunting up and inventing new modes of preparing it for consumption, as well as appropriating unheard of articles as food. I recollect even "saw-dust" was attempted to be converted into bread, while horse-beans were cooked in all sorts of ways to be made palatable, and were also ground down to a sort of flour as a substitute for wheat. The newspapers teemed with cautions to the public to use the utmost economy, while recipes without end appeared as to how bad flour could be best used and made wholesome. It will scarcely be credited that even a public notice emanated from the Town Hall on this subject, signed by Mr. Statham, the Town Clerk. I have by me a copy of it, which, as it may interest some of my readers, I will give entire. It is headed—

### JOHN WRIGHT, MAYOR.

### MAKING OF BREAD.

### NOTICE TO HOUSEKEEPERS,
and dealers in flour.

Complaints having been made against some of the Flour Dealers in this town for having sold Flour unfit for the making of Bread, the Mayor thinks proper to acquaint the Public that, upon an investigation of such complaints, it appeared that in many instances blame was not imputable to the Flour Dealer, but to the Purchaser of the Flour in not having taken proper precautions in the Making of the Bread, which, owing to the state of the Flour this season, it was necessary to have taken, and which had been pointed out to the party by the Flour Dealer.

From the above circumstance, the Mayor has been induced to recommend to all Dealer's in Flour upon the Sale of any Flour which, although not unsound, may render proper precautions necessary in the use of the same, to apprise their several customers thereof; and the Mayor has been further induced to recommend to all Housekeepers the adoption of the following system in the Making of Bread:—

To boil the water and let it stand till of a proper heat, to knead the Flour well, using as little water as possible, and let it stand a sufficient time to rise; to use fresh Water Barm, and bake the Bread on the oven bottom, in small loaves of not more than 2lb. to 3lb. weight; to use, as much as possible, Cakes or Hard Bread, and not to use the Bread new.

By Order of the Mayor,
STATHAM, Town Clerk.

22 *Nov.* 1816.

In London the distress was so great that the people there were full of a rebellious element; at a meeting in Spitalfields, whereat the celebrated, or, if the term be more appropriate, "notorious," Henry Hunt was present, and addressed a numerous assembly, frightful disorders took place. Meetings of large bodies of the people were held in all the leading cities and towns throughout the kingdom to petition the Prince Regent and parliament to do something effectual to stay the tide of calamity that seemed to be setting steadily in to overwhelm the nation.

The petition from Liverpool was most numerously and respectably signed; and I recollect that so determined were the memorialists to ascertain whether their petition had been properly presented that a correspondence took place on the subject and was made public, between his worship the mayor, Sir W. Barton, and General Gascoigne, one of our members, relative to its having reached its destination.

The price of wheat in the month of December, 1816, was 21s. per 70lbs., while the quartern loaf of 4lb. 5oz. cost 1s. 6¾d. The penny loaf only weighed 3oz. 1¼ dr.

To the credit of the working classes in Liverpool, the utmost patience and forbearance was exhibited under intense sufferings. I recollect well the energy exhibited by the gentry of the town, in their endeavours to raise funds for the general relief. The Dock Trustees employed numbers of people at 2s. a day. A large loan was raised to enable them to give unlimited employment. The leading firms in the town were subscribers to this loan, which was headed by the Norwich Union Life and Fire Office with £1000. In the churches and chapels charity sermons were constantly preached, and the clergy of all denominations urged their flocks to give anything at all, and not to withhold even their mites.

Gentlemen formed themselves into parties to canvass subscriptions for the poor from house to house, while the ladies left no stone unturned to further the cause of charity. It was a most remarkable epoch in the history of this country, and certainly in Liverpool the time was as trying as could possibly be conceived. Merchants and tradesmen were daily failing. Great houses, apparently able to stand any amount of pressure, gave way, and many of the provincial banks succumbed, adding to the horrors of the time. Amongst other schemes afloat to relieve distress in Liverpool was the benefit got up at the Theatre Royal, to which I have referred. The prices of admission were doubled on the occasion. The box tickets were 9s., the upper boxes, 8s., the pit, 6s., and the gallery, 2s.; and the proceeds realised no less a sum than £610! The performances were the "Poor Gentleman," "A Concert," by musical amateurs, and the burlesque of "Bombastes Furioso." The characters were personated for the most part in each of the pieces by amateurs, amongst whom were several of the leading gentlemen of the town, who spared no pains, study, nor cost to render their exertions successful.

There may be still left amongst us some of those who took part in the glory of that memorable evening of Saturday, December 7, 1816. At this distant time, they may still indulge in a feeling of pride at their successful endeavours to further a good cause, and they will not, I am sure, be offended at an old man recording the amount of talent they exhibited, nor the zeal they manifested in fully carrying out the plan proposed for the public amusement and the welfare of the poor. I recollect there was an admirably written prologue, by Dr. Shepherd, which was as admirably delivered by Mr. J. H. Parr, in the character of *Stephen Harrowby*, a character which he personated in the play with all the finish of an experienced actor, his exertions drawing forth frequent and loud applause. *Dr. Ollapod* was personated by Dr. Carter, who excited roars of laughter.

I recollect the names of Messrs. Aldridge, Bartleman, Cooper, Greaves, Halewood, Hime, Jackson (a distinguished violoncello player, by the way), Langhorne, Maybrick, Tayleure (a distinguished double bass), and Vaughan. In "Bombastes Furioso," *King Artaxomines* was personated by Mr. Richmond; *Fusbos* by Mr. Clay; *General Bombastes* by Mr. J. H. Parr, who elicited shouts of laughter by his drollery and admirable acting. Miss Grant, of the Theatre Royal Company, played *Distaffina*. The house was crowded in every part, the whole town seemed to take an interest in the matter, and every nerve was strained to command success. In fact so well did those who had undertaken the disposal of tickets succeed, that numbers of persons could not gain admission although possessing tickets, while hundreds who in vain crowded round the doors were unable to obtain entrance "for love or money." A more cordial display of goodwill was never known in this town, nor was there ever a more enthusiastic, elegant, or better pleased audience assembled within the walls of the Theatre Royal than on that occasion.

At this time there was considerable ferment in the public mind, relative to, and consequent upon, the escape of Lord Cochrane from the King's Bench prison, and when the gallant and noble lord was re-captured and re-committed with a fine of £100 inflicted upon him, the men of Liverpool were early astir in the noble sailor's behalf—a subscription box was opened instantly the matter became known in Liverpool, and it was resolved that not more than a "penny" should be given by each person towards the fine, and each subscriber should, on payment of his money, sign his name and address. A shop at the corner of John-street and Dale-street, was one place appointed for the reception of pence and names, while another was in Mersey-street opposite the end of Liver-street. Crowds of persons were assembled round these places who loudly and admiringly canvassed the noble lord's conduct. He was quite the hero of his day, and in no place had his lordship more enthusiastic admirers than in Liverpool amongst the liberal party. By the people generally, he was quite idolized. In a very short time 2500 pence and names were obtained, and had 25,000 been wanted, I am sure they would have been as readily subscribed. As it may be interesting to some of my readers to know how the £100 fine was paid, I can give them some particulars thereupon, £85 was paid in bank notes, £5 in silver, and £10 in copper. It was said in a joke, that if the whole amount had been tendered in brass it would have been readily accepted, so glad were authorities to get rid of so troublesome a customer.

# CHAPTER XIV.

On Sunday morning, February 11, 1810, I was standing in St. Nicholas churchyard, in company with two old friends. We were waiting the arrival of the congregation, and the commencement of the morning service. The second bells were chiming. We had been looking on the river with that interest which is always felt in gazing upon such a scene. Our conversation had turned upon the benefits which a good sound Christian education must confer upon the lower classes of society. Education at the period to which I refer was then beginning to take hold of the public mind, as an essential to the well-doing of the people. This subject in later years, as is known, has become an absorbing question. Our remarks had been evoked by the neat appearance of the children of the Moorfields Schools, who had just passed near where we stood, as they entered the church. One of us remarked in reference to the Tower close by, that it was the dower of the Lady Blanche, the daughter of John O'Gaunt, who, although occupying so eminently marked a place in history, was a man so narrow-minded that he would not allow any of his vassals to receive the least education as he held that it unfitted them for the duties of their station, and gave them ideas far above their lot in life. A curious speculation was hazarded by one of my friend's that as Water-street was anciently called "Bank-street," whether the word "Bank" ought not to have been "Blanche"-street; a name given to it in honour of the lady to whom the principal building in the street belonged, when, just as he had finished speaking, we heard, as if above us, a smart crack. On looking round to ascertain the cause, a sight burst upon our view, that none who witnessed it could ever forget. The instant we turned, we beheld the church tower give way, on the south-west side, and immediately afterwards the spire fell with a frightful and appalling crash into the body of the building. The spire seemed at first to topple over, and then it dropped perpendicularly like a pack of cards into a solid heap, burying everything, as may be supposed, below it. There were many persons in the churchyard, waiting to enter the sacred edifice, and, like ourselves, were struck dumb with horror and dismay at the frightful catastrophe. We were soon aroused to a state of consciousness, and inaction gave way to exertion. In a very short time, the noise of the crash had brought hundreds of persons into the churchyard to ascertain the cause. Amidst the rising dust were heard the dreadful screams of the poor children who had become involved in the ruins; and not long after, their screams were added to by the frantic exclamations of parents and friends who, in an incredibly short time had hurried to the scene of the disaster. Crowds of people rushed into the churchyard, some hurrying to and fro, scarcely knowing what to fear or what to do. That the children were to be exhumed was an immediate thought, and as immediately carried into execution. Men of all ranks were seen, quite regardless of their Sunday clothes, busily employed in removing the ruins—gentlemen, merchants, tradesmen, shopmen and apprentices, willingly aiding the sturdy labourers in their good work, and, in a short time, first one little sufferer, and then another, was dragged out from the mass of stone and brick and timber that lay in a confused heap. Twenty-eight little ones were at length brought out, of whom twenty-three were dead; five were alive, and were taken to the Infirmary, but of these, only three survived. They were horribly maimed, and so disfigured that they were scarcely recognizable. These twenty-eight poor little bodies were at first laid in rows in the churchyard to be claimed by their parents and friends, many of whom were to be seen running to and fro looking distracted with the great calamity that had befallen them. Of all the pitiable sights I ever beheld, the sight of these little things laid on the grass was the most piteous; and, as, one by one they were claimed and taken away—in some instances parents claiming two, and in one instance, three children—the utmost sympathy was felt for those who had been so suddenly bereft.

It was most fortunate that the accident did not occur half an hour—nay, a quarter of an hour—later, or the calamity might have been such as would have marked the day as one of the darkest in our annals—a frightful spot in our calendar. Beside the children, there were only about twenty people seated in the church, far from the scene of the disaster, and they, on the first indication of danger, had fled and sought safety outside the building. How the bell-ringers escaped, it is impossible to tell, but escape they did, and that unhurt, with the exception of one, who rushed back to get his clothes and was killed. It was to their intense stupidity and obstinacy that this catastrophe may be ascribed. Previous to the accident, they had been told that the tower was unsafe, and on that very morning, they were advised not to ring the bells again, until an examination of the building had taken place: but ring they would, and ring they did, and the result of their ringing was a death-knell unmatched in local history.

Nor were the authorities altogether free from blame. It was said that they were apprised of the insecurity of the tower, and yet did not take steps to avoid the accident. The escapes of people on their way to church were wonderful, and many traced their good fortune to being tardy in getting ready, or from leaving home at an usually late moment. The scene of the disaster was for a long time an attraction to people residing miles from Liverpool, and the country around sent thousands to gaze on the unusual sight presented to their view.

In the same year the sad calamity I have just recorded took place, the Theatre Royal was the scene of a frightful disturbance, which ended in the trial at Lancaster of several highly respectable men, for being partakers in it. I have a distinct recollection of this affair, and a more disgraceful one to all parties concerned in it, cannot be imagined. These riots were termed the H. P. riots.

In the September of the preceding year there had been considerable agitation in the theatrical world of London, and dreadful riots had taken place as to the old prices, and the question was whether new and advanced prices should be charged for admission to the theatres. A number of individuals, as many as forty, were tried for the offence of rioting at Covent Garden, when, to the surprise of everyone, the whole of the party were found "Not guilty."

There is no doubt that this strange verdict in reference to most outrageous and unjustifiable conduct had put it into the heads of many people in Liverpool that similar conduct might be indulged in, with like impunity, respecting the Theatre Royal. There had been frequent attempts made to induce the lessees of the theatre, Messrs. Lewis and Knight, to permit a half-price to be taken. The plea for the request was that numbers of persons who would like occasionally to visit a theatre were debarred doing so from the fact that their hours of employment were so late that they could not get away in time to attend when the performances commenced, and they thought it a hard case that they should be obliged to pay full price for only half the quantity of amusement. The lessees pleaded their expenses were just the same, whether the people came at full price or half-price, and since the Theatre Royal had been established no such arrangement had been attempted, and as it would not pay them to concede a half price they declined to do so. They said their undertaking in the theatre was a private speculation for a public purpose, and they had no right to be compelled to do, what no other tradesmen would be expected to do, that is, prosecute their business at a loss. The play-goers, however, seemed determined to carry things with a high hand, and endeavour to force Messrs. Lewis and Knight to come to their terms. The season was announced to commence on the 11th of May, 1810, when there appeared, a few days previously, on the walls of the town the following placard:—

THE THEATRE OPENS
ON MONDAY NEXT, 11TH MAY.

THE MANAGERS
Have been requested to permit admission at

HALF-PRICE,

As in London, etc. (and elsewhere), but they still persist in
the injustice of demanding FULL PRICES, from those who
have it not in their power to attend until a very late hour,
when a good and material part of the performance is over!
We have even a greater right to the indulgence than the
London audiences—

LET US
BOLDLY CLAIM IT
AND
WE MUST SUCCEED!!

This placard was followed by others. An abusive letter also made its
appearance, as well as a pamphlet equally offensive, in which the lessees
were held up to scorn, ridicule, and opprobrium. In fact, every step was
taken to excite the (play-going) public mind on the subject of "half-price or
full-price."

When the opening night arrived, crowds of people assembled outside
the theatre, and the rush to get in, when the doors opened, was immense.
Numbers of places had been previously taken in the boxes, by persons
who were seen to be most actively engaged in the riots in the theatre
afterwards. No sooner had the curtain rose to the play of "Pizarro" than
the row began—shoutings, bawlings, whistlings, hornblowings, turnings of
rattles, flappings of clappers, and every noise that could be made by the
human voice was indulged in, and the uproar seemed to increase as the
night went on—such a scene of confusion can hardly be conceived, and
amidst the turbulence that reigned placards were exhibited demanding
"half-price." In vain the managers attempted to obtain a hearing—in vain
favourite actors came forward, hoping to be heard—the play proceeded,
but all in "inexplicable dumb show and noise." These riots were repeated
on the nights of the 14th and 16th, when it was found necessary to close
the theatre. Each night the same riotous behaviour was exhibited. In fact,
to such an extent had it arrived that the Mayor was at length sent for, and
read the Riot Act. The mob outside threw brick-bats, stones, and all sorts of
missiles at the windows, which they completely smashed, breaking away
even the woodwork of the frames. The people outside kept bawling "Half-

price!" and when any of the known adherents of the full price attempted to get out of the theatre they were driven back and insulted, while those in favour of "Half-price" were cheered and applauded most vociferously. At length, it was determined by the magistrates that the strong arm of the law should be stretched out, and in consequence, six persons who had been most active in the disturbances were arrested, and brought to trial at the autumn assizes at Lancaster, for conspiracy and riot. These delinquents were all gentlemen of position in the town, and, as may be supposed, the case excited the utmost attention and interest. The case was tried on the 14th September. Sir Robert Graham was the judge. I remember Serjeant Cockle was for the prosecution, assisted by Messrs. Park, Topping, Holroyd, and Clark, nearly all of whom, by the way, I think, have since obtained seats on the judicial bench. The council for the defence were Messrs. Raine, Scarlett (afterwards Sir James Scarlett), Raincock, and Richardson. Sergeant Cockle, in opening the case highly lauded Messrs. Lewis and Banks as actors, men, and citizens, and pointed out to the jury how monstrous the conduct of the prisoners had been, in attempting to force an unprofitable movement upon anyone. I recollect he made use of this remarkable expression, "that every person resorting to a theatre has a right to express his dissatisfaction against any thing he sees, either of the plays performed or the actors, and that he must do this honestly: but if he conspire with others to damn any play or condemn any actor, punishment should follow such conspiracy."

At the trial Mr. Statham, the Town Clerk, gave also evidence for the prosecution. After the court had been occupied some time, and many witnesses had been examined, an attempt was made on the part of the judge to effect a compromise, His Lordship remarking that he thought the ends of justice had been served in the public exposure and annoyance which the defendants had been put to, and that as the temper of the people had subsided, and even a better understanding existed between the public and the lessees than before, he thought it was of no use to carry the case any further. The council for the prosecution, however, would not consent to this; at the same time they assured the judge and the court, that the prosecution was not carried on by the lessees, but by the magistrates of the borough, who were determined to put a stop, by all means in their power, to a recurrence of such disgraceful proceedings, and attempts on the part of an unthinking public to force gentlemen to do what they did not consider right or equitable. The verdict returned was "guilty of riot, but not of conspiracy."

# CHAPTER XV.

I have never been much of a play-goer, but have occasionally visited the theatres when remarkable performers have appeared. I recollect many of the leading actors and actresses of the close of the last century, while all the great ones of this I have seen from time to time. Joe Munden, Incledon, Braham, Fawcett, Michael Kelly, Mrs. Crouch, Mrs. Siddons, Madame Catalani Booth, and Cooke, and all the bright stars who have been ennobled—Miss Farrell (Lady Derby), Miss Bolton (Lady Thurlow), Miss Stephens (Countess of Essex), Miss Love (Lady Harboro), Miss Foote (Marchioness Harrington), Miss Mellon (Duchess of St. Alban's), Miss O'Neil (Lady Beecher)—but I must say the old and the new style of acting, appear to be very different. Mrs. Siddons exhibited the highest perfection of acting. I cannot conceive anything that can go beyond it in dramatic art.

I was present when John Kemble bade farewell to the Liverpool audiences. It took place in the summer of 1813. The play was "Coriolanus." The house was crowded to excess, and the utmost enthusiasm was exhibited in favour of the great tragedian; who, although not a townsman, was at any rate a county man, he having been born at Prescot.

Mr. Kemble, when addressing the audience on that occasion, made a very remarkable declaration. He said that "it was on the Liverpool stage he first adapted the play of 'Coriolanus,' and produced it, as they had just seen it performed, and that it was the earnest encouragement he then received that proved a great stimulus to him in after life."

A statement of the sums of money received at benefits amongst the "old stagers" may perhaps interest some of my readers. I am going back a long way, but I do so that those who know or who guess at the receipts of the "moderns" may compare them with those of the "ancients." In 1795 Mrs. Maddocks, a most delightful actress, and an immense favourite in Liverpool, drew £213; Mrs. Powell, £207; Mr Banks, £183; Mr. Whitfield, £135. Mr. Kelly, the Irish singer, and Mrs. Crouch, a most charming and fascinating woman, with a lovely voice, realised together £136; Mr. Hollinsworth, £124; and Mr. Ward £119. In modern days the Clarkes (the manager and his wife) have received as much as £300 at their benefits. One of the best speculations Mr. Lewis ever made was the engagement of Paganini, shortly after his first appearance in the metropolis, in, I think, 1829 or 1830. This wonderful genius had taken the musical world of London by storm, and struck terror and despair into the hearts of the violinists of his day; one and all of whom declaring, as a friend of mine said of his own playing—although eminent in his profession—"that they were only fiddlers." Paganini's playing was most unearthly and inhuman. I never heard anything like the tones he produced from his violin—the sounds now crashing as if a demoniac was tearing and straining at the strings, now melting away with the softest and tenderest harmonies. He kept his hearers enthralled by his magical music, and astonished by his wonderful execution. I shall never forget hearing him play the "Walpurgis Nacht," when he appeared at the Amphitheatre in 1835 or 1836. It was painting a picture by means of sounds. His descriptive powers were wonderful. Anybody with the least touch of imagination could bring before "his mind's eye" the infernal revel that the artist was depicting. The enchantments of the witches were visible. You could hear their diabolical songs, you could fancy their mad and wild dances; while, when the cock crew (imitated by the way in a most astonishing manner), you would feel that there was a rushing of bodies through the air, which were scattering in all directions. Then the lovely melody succeeding— descriptive of the calm dawn of summer morning—came soothingly on the senses after the strain of excitement that the mind had experienced. In that delicious melody you could fancy you saw the rosy colours of the breaking day and gradually the rising of the sun, giving light and beauty to the world. That performance was the most wonderful I ever listened to, and I feel confident no one but those who did hear this strange man can ever entertain any notion of his style or performance. His first engagement in Liverpool was at the Theatre Royal, and a characteristic anecdote is related of the Signor in this transaction. At the Amphitheatre, Signor De Begnis, the great harp player—the husband of the fascinating Ronzi de Begnis, and who ran away with Lady Bishop, (he was the ugliest man for a Cavaliero I ever saw, being deeply pitted with the smallpox)—had been giving some concerts which were exceedingly unsuccessful. The people engaged got no money, De. Begnis having completely failed in the speculation. The news of this having reached London, Paganini heard of it, and when Mr. Lewis proposed to engage him, he jumped at the conclusion that this was the same as De Begnis's speculation and that there could be only one theatre in Liverpool. He accordingly declined to come to Liverpool, unless the money to be paid to him was first lodged at his bankers (Messrs. Coutts) in London. Mr. Lewis saw through the Signor's error at once, and immediately remitted £1000 to ratify the engagement for ten nights. Paganini played his ten nights and drew on each of them from £280 to £300, so that, great as the risk was, the speculation was a most advantageous one to the lessee. When Paganini came to the Amphitheatre in 1835 or '36 (I think) with Watson as his manager, and Miss Watson as his *Cantatrice*, he did not draw as on his first appearance, although the houses were very good. I recollect talking to Mr. Watson on the stage between the parts, when the gods, growing impatient, whistled loudly for a re-commencement of the performance. Paganini, who happened to be near us, seemed rather surprised at the noise, and turning to Watson he inquired *qu'est que c'est ces tapageurs ces siffleurs?* and on being told, he grinned horribly, and said in a low voice—*Bah! betes!*

I once was told, by one of the actors employed at the Theatre Royal, a curious anecdote of a remarkable and distinguished lady. I don't recollect the year it happened, but I think it must have been about 1829. In that year a carriage drove up to the Theatre Royal, containing two ladies, attended by a man-servant in green and gold livery. The servant went into the theatre to inquire if Mr. Clarke, the stage-manager, was in. On being answered in the affirmative, the stoutest of the two ladies—for the other lady was quite young—stepped out of the carriage, and without ceremony walked through the lobby straight upon the stage, to the utter surprise of the hall-keeper who, like a masonic tyler, allows no one to pass without a word or sign of recognition that they are of the privileged. The man followed the lady, who, stepping to the footlights, gazed around on that most desolate of all desolate, dreary, dingy places, the inside of a theatre by daylight. On her still handsome countenance alternated emotions of pride, regretful feeling, as well as of deep interest. After looking across the pit for a few moments, she turned to the hall-porter and requested him to announce to Mr. Clarke that a lady wished to see him for a few minutes. The man quickly returned, requesting the lady to follow him, but she, passing him, made her way to the treasury with the air and mien of one who well knew the way to that place of torture when a "ghost does not walk." The lady accosted Mr. Clarke with a winning air, and seeing that she was not recognised, said, "So you don't recollect me?" "No, indeed, I do not." "Well, that is strange, considering the money you have paid me. Why," she continued, "do you not recollect who played *Little Pickle* at Swansea and Bristol in 18--?" "Bless me!" exclaimed Mr. Clarke. "Ah! I see you know me now," said the lady laughing. "And many a week's salary I have had there," continued the buxom visitor, pointing to the pay-place, "and now just let me have something paid to me to remind me of old times." Whereupon she went to the pay-place, when the gallant stage-manager put down a week's salary as of old, which the lady took up, returning it however, and placing at the same time in Mr. Clarke's hand, a note for £20, which she desired him to distribute amongst the most needy of the company. The lady was the Duchess of St. Alban's. When Miss Mellon, she had been engaged at the Theatre Royal, and the first benefit she had was in Liverpool. I knew a gentleman who exerted himself greatly on her behalf on that occasion, and the success of it was mainly attributable to his efforts. This she always gratefully acknowledged, and I recollect his telling me that once, being in London, this admirable and kind-hearted lady—who so worthily used the wealth at her command, after she was ennobled—recognised him while passing down Pall Mall and beckoned him to the side of her magnificent equipage, and there recalled the old time to his recollection acknowledging the old obligation, assuring him that if she could in any way serve him she would be delighted to do so.

The Theatre Royal, about forty odd years ago was under the lesseeship of Messrs. Lewis and Banks. Mr. Banks was extremely fond of a good and well-dressed dish; he had a person as cook who had been with him some years, and who suited his taste in his most choice dishes. The two had a serious quarrel, which ended in cooky giving her master notice of leaving his service. Mr. Banks took this somewhat to heart as he thought if he parted with his cook—and such a cook as she was—he might not be able to replace her. To put it out of her power to give him notice again, he offered her marriage, and was accepted. Mrs. Banks sometimes used to visit the theatre, and generally took her seat at the wing by the prompter's table, where she could see tolerably well what was going forward on the stage. On one occasion the tragedy of "Venice Preserved" was being performed. Edmund Kean was *Jaffier* and Miss O'Neil *Belvidera*. They were playing to a greatly excited house, as may well be supposed when two such artists were upon the stage. Mr. St. A---, who was then ballet-master at the theatre, and who, by the way, was a most graceful dancer, seeing Mrs. Banks, went up to her to exchange compliments. Having done so, Mr. St. A--- remarked how seldom they had the pleasure of seeing Mrs. Banks. "Oh," replied she, "I never come to the theatre—not I. There's no good actors now-a-days—there ain't anybody worth seeing." "Dear me, Mrs, B., how can you say so? Who have we on the stage now? There's Mr. Kean"—"Mr. Kean, indeed," exclaimed Mrs. B., "I can't abide him; he's my abortion." "Well, then, what do you think of Miss O'Neil?" "Miss O'Neil!—Miss O'Neil, indeed; do you call her a hactress?—I can't abide her. There she is—see how she lolls and lollups on the fellows—it's quite disgusting!" Now the fact was that Miss O'Neil who was chastity itself off the stage, and who lead a most blameless life, showed, when performing, such *abandon* and *impressment* in her actions as to be quite remarkable, especially in parts where the intensity of passion had to be displayed, and this Mrs. Banks "couldn't abide." "Well, then," continued Mr. St. A---, "who do you call a good actor?" "Who do I call a good actor! you wait till my dear John Emery comes down, and then you'll see a good actor; and if I live as long, I'll make him such a pudding, please

God, as he hasn't had this many a day!" Old Mrs. Banks was about right as to John Emery; he was an actor of the first-class, and has never been replaced in his peculiar line. I have seen Emery play *Tyke* in the "School of Reform." It was a wonderful impersonation. I have seen nothing like it since.

It has always appeared to me to be a remarkable circumstance that many actors and actresses who have been great favourites in the metropolis, have not stood in the same light with the Liverpool audiences. I have seen, occasionally, some remarkable instances of this. Dowton, a great actor, never drew; James Wallack never attracted large audiences. I have seen the whole Adelphi company—including Frederick Yates, his charming wife, Paul Bedford, John Reeve, O. Smith, and others—fail to draw; in fact at one engagement they played night after night to almost empty benches. This was, I think, in 1838. I recollect, on one occasion, Yates seeing a band-box on the stage, went up to it and gave it a kick, and looking significantly at the state of the house, exclaimed, "Get out of my sight—I hate empty boxes!"

Vandenhoff was always a great favourite with the Liverpool audiences. There was a tremendous row once got up at the Theatre Royal, in which he was concerned. About 1825, I think, Vandenhoff went to try his fortune on the London stage, and there, if he did not altogether fail, he did not succeed commensurate with his great expectations; and after knocking about at several theatres, playing, I believe, at some of the minors—the Surrey, Coburg, and Sadler's Wells—he came back to Liverpool, where a Mr. Salter had taken up the position he had vacated. A strong move by Mr. Vandenhoff's friends was made to reinstate him on the Liverpool Tragic Throne. This Mr. Salter's friends would not allow. The consequence was that several noisy demonstrations took place on both sides, and considerable confusion was created during the time the row was kept up. To show to what length things went, I may just mention that placards were freely exhibited in the theatre bearing the sentiments on them of the particular side which exhibited them. I recollect one caused great fun and laughter. It was headed "Vandenhoff" and "Salter-off."

Kean thought highly of Vandenhoff. I have seen a letter of his in which he highly extols him, considering his style to be the purest acting since the retirement of John Kemble.

In the autumn of 1824, there was a great row at the Theatre Royal, which was excited in favour of Miss Cramer, a most popular and able vocalist. At that time the Music Hall in Bold-street had just been opened, and concerts were being given under the management of Mr. Wilson, the dancing master, whose niece by the way (Miss Bolton) was married to John Braham, *il primo tenore d'Europa*, as the Italians termed him. Braham has often said that this

Music Hall was a finer room for sound than any that ever he was in; and at these morning concerts he frequently sang. It was the custom to enlist the aid of the vocalists, if there were any, at the Theatre Royal, to add to the attractions of these concerts. The manager was always willing to allow his singers to avail themselves of the occasion. However, on Miss Cramer being offered an engagement, the manager refused to allow her to appear. Miss Cramer, feeling the injustice of the case, nevertheless sang at one of the morning concerts, and was consequently dismissed from the Theatre Royal. The young lady instantly issued a handbill stating her case, and the consequence was that the theatre was crowded at night, and calls for "Miss Cramer" were incessant. Mr. Banks came forward to justify himself, hoping that both sides might be heard, but he could not obtain a hearing. At length the audience grew so excited that they tore up the seats, smashed a splendid chandelier that had only just been purchased at a cost of £500, broke all the windows in the house, and did a great deal of damage. The row was continued on the night but one following, when other damage was effected, and it was only by closing the theatre for a few days that peace could be restored. Some of the rioters were afterwards tried at Lancaster, and, I think, heavily fined.

# CHAPTER XVI.

In the year 1816, in consequence of the high price of provisions, as mentioned in a former chapter, many persons rendered desperate by their wants, formed themselves into gangs of robbers, and committed many daring acts of depredation. Travellers were constantly stopped, ill-treated, and robbed on the roads in the vicinity of the town; and scarcely a day passed, without intelligence arriving of some house in the outskirts being attacked and plundered. To such an extent was this carried, that people commenced forming themselves into associations for their mutual protection. In Toxteth Park, this was especially the case, as several very serious robberies had been reported in that neighbourhood. It must be remembered that at that time Toxteth Park was but thinly populated. There were only a few good houses in it, occupied by highly respectable families, for the salubrious air of "the Park," and the beautiful views of the river from many parts of it, gave it attractions to those who could live out of town. It was, amongst other things, proposed, I recollect, to have as protection, large and sonorous bells put up on the tops of the houses, so that on the least alarm of thieves, the bells might be rung to arouse the neighbours. Such precautions will be laughed at now-a-days, but something was necessary to be done at that time, when policemen were unknown, and personal protection was by no means much regarded. It was no uncommon circumstance for persons who had occasion to go out at night, to carry a brace of pistols with them; but whether they would have had courage to use them or not, I cannot say, but the fact of having such things at hand were crumbs of comfort to timid people.

I dare say many of my readers will remember having seen in old carriages and gigs, a sort of round projection at the back, forming a recess from the inside of the vehicle. These boxes were used for the purpose of depositing therein a sword and pistols, so that they might be ready at hand in case of necessity.

The extent to which robbery was committed in Liverpool at this period, may be judged by the following circumstance, which many may still remember. On the particulars being made public people were completely terrified at the state to which things had arrived, and several families living in the suburbs, seriously thought of returning to reside in the town again.

About the month of August, 1816, an old woman was seen prowling constantly about the vicinity of Mr. J. A. Yates' house, in Toxteth Park. She made a great many inquiries about the members of that gentleman's family, whether there were men servants in the house, and whether a dog was kept. In fact, she made herself fully acquainted with Mr. Yates' domestic arrangements. This was thought nothing of at the time, but the old crone's curiosity was recalled to mind after the event took place, which I shall briefly mention.

On the night of Friday, 16th August, 1816, about ten o'clock, six men wearing masks, and armed with pistols, might have been seen approaching Mr. Yates' house. Two of them took their position outside as sentinels to give alarm to their companions, if necessary. The other four approached the back of the premises, and entered the house. Passing through the scullery they went into the kitchen, where they found a servant-maid and a footman. Threatening them with instant death if they gave any alarm, one of the four remained in the kitchen to watch the girl, while the other three compelled the footman to show them over the house. Proceeding up stairs, they encountered Mr. J. B. Yates, who was on a visit to Mr. J. A. Yates. On seeing the men approach, he inquired their business, when one of them aimed a blow at him, which, however, fortunately missed its mark, and only inflicted a slight wound on Mr. Yates's mouth. They then ordered Mr. Yates to give up his money, which he did, fearing further violence. Driving him before them, they next entered a room, in which Mrs. J. B. Yates was sitting. They compelled her also to give up her money, watch, and the jewellery she wore. While this was going on, Mr. J. A. Yates arrived from Liverpool, and was seized by the two rascals stationed outside. They demanded his money, putting pistols to his head. Mr. Yates, however, with a good deal of nerve, rushed past the fellows, threw his watch away, and seized hold of the handle of the door bell, which he rung with considerable force. The men, however, again seized him, and told him his ringing would be of no use, as there were fellows inside who could overmaster any effort of his. But the ringing of the door-bell had seriously alarmed the party within, who were then robbing Mrs. Yates, as just mentioned. Snatching up whatever they could, which was portable and seemed of value, the fellows rushed down stairs, ordering the footman to open the hall-door. This he did, and availed himself of the opportunity of making his escape. He ran across the fields and speedily gave an alarm, but too late to be of any service; for, when assistance arrived, the thieves had decamped, taking with them about £14 in money, and a quantity of valuable plate and jewellery. The man left in the kitchen had contrived to secure the stock of plate. Four of the robbers were captured in September following, and committed to take their trial at Lancaster, where they were found guilty and sentenced to death. They were hung in October following, and it is a rather curious circumstance that the very week these men suffered the extreme penalty of the law for their misdeeds, a daring burglary was committed one night at the mill near Mr. Yates' house, when five sacks of flour were stolen, put into a boat in waiting by the mill dam, and successfully carried off.

The Waterloo Hotel was originally Mr. Gore's house. It was afterwards occupied by Mr. Staniforth, who was in partnership with the present Mr. Laird's father as ropers. The roperies occupied the site of the present Arcades, and extended to Berry-street.

I recollect the Fall Well occupying the site of Mr. Alderman Bennet's warehouse near Rose-street. It was covered over with several arches; access to it was obtained down a flight of steps. A tavern was afterwards built on its site, and was known for many years as the "Fall Well Tavern." It stood at the corner of Rose-street at the back of the Amphitheatre. The Dye-House Well was in Greetham-street. I believe access is still obtained to the water, at least it was a few years ago. The wells on Shaw's brow were all laid open when the alteration took place in that vicinity. One of the wells was used at an emery mill, which was once the cone of a pottery. One of the wells was found where the Library is now erected.

# CHAPTER XVII.

As a young boy and an old man I have seen my native town under two very diverse aspects.

As a boy, I have seen it ranked only as a third-rate seaport. Its streets tortuous and narrow, with pavements in the middle, skirted by mud or dirt as the season happened. The sidewalks rough with sharp-pointed stones, that made it misery to walk upon them. I have seen houses, with little low rooms, suffice for the dwelling of the merchant or well-to-do trader—the first being content to live in Water-street or Old Hall-street, while the latter had no idea of leaving his little shop, with its bay or square window, to take care of itself at night. I have seen Liverpool streets with scarcely a coach or vehicle in them, save such as trade required, and the most enlightened of its inhabitants, at that time, could not boast of much intelligence, while those who constituted its lower orders were plunged in the deepest vice, ignorance, and brutality.

But we should not judge too harshly of those who have gone before us. Of the sea-savouring greatly were the friends and acquaintances of my youth. Scarcely a town by the margin of the ocean could be more salt in its people than the men of Liverpool of the last century: so barbarous were they in their amusements, bull-baitings and cock and dog-fightings, and pugilistic encounters. What could we expect when we opened no book to the young, and employed no means of imparting knowledge to the old?—deriving our prosperity from two great sources—the slave-trade and privateering. What could we expect but the results we have witnessed? Swarming with sailor men flushed with prize money, was it not likely that the inhabitants generally would take a tone from what they daily beheld and quietly countenanced? Have we not seen the father investing small sums in some gallant ship fitting out for the West Indies or the Spanish Main, in the names of each of his children, girls and boys? Was it not natural that they should go down to the "Old Dock," or the "Salthouse," or the "New Dock," and there be gratified with a sight of a ship of which they—little as they were—were still part-owners? We took them on deck and showed them where a bloody battle had been fought—on the very deck and spot on which their little feet pattered about. And did we not show them the very guns, and the muskets, the pistols and the cutlasses, the shot-lockers and magazines, and tell them how the lad, scrubbing a brass kettle in the caboose, had been occupied as a powder-monkey and seen blood shed in earnest? And did we not moreover tell them that if the forthcoming voyage was only successful, and if the ships of the enemy were taken—no matter about the streams of blood that might run through the scuppers—how their little ventures would be raised in value many hundredfold—would not young imaginations be excited and the greed for gain be potent in their young hearts? No matter what woman might be widowed—parent made childless, or child left without protector—if the gallant privateer was successful that was all they were taught to look for. And must not such teaching have had effect in after life? I have seen these things, and know them to be true; but I have seen them, I am glad to say, fade away, while other and better prospects have, step by step, presented themselves to view.

As a man, I have seen the old narrow streets widening—the old houses crumbling—and the salty savouring of society evaporate, and the sea influence recede before improvement—education and enlightenment of all sorts. Step by step has that sea-element in my townsmen declined. The three-bottle and punch-drinking man is the exception now, and not the rule of the table. The wide, open street and the ample window is now everywhere to be found, while underneath that street the well-constructed sewer carries off the germs of disease that in other times rose up potently amongst us, and through that window comes streaming the sunlight of heaven, cheering and gladdening every heart. Scarcely can the man of old, who has outlived his generation, believe in the huge edifices that now the merchant occupies, or credit his sight, when he looks at the great shops that display their costly goods of all descriptions, with the best of taste. Nor is there a less remarkable aspect presented in the appearance of the people. Of old one scarcely met a well-dressed man—now scores upon scores. In bye-gone times, we scarcely beheld a carriage, lumbering and uneasy as those things were—now we see elegant equipages of every make, shape, and build, suitable for every style of locomotion. In all things have we progressed; nor are we yet standing still.

We are doubling our trade. We are doubling our imports and exports; we have been doubling them since 1749—about every 16 years. In that year the total tonnage of vessels that entered the port of Liverpool was 28,250 tons. In 1764 it was 56,499 tons, in 1780 it was 112,000 tons, in 1796 it was 224,000 tons, in 1811 it was 611,190 tons, in 1827 it was 1,225,313 tons, in 1841 it was 2,425,461 tons, in 1857 it had reached 4,645,362 tons, so that by the same rule that doubled the tonnage of the port, between 1749 and 1764, the tonnage doubled itself between 1841 and 1857. It occupied 134 years to produce an increase equal to that which had taken place between 1841 and 1857. The value of exports in the whole kingdom in 1857, amounted to £110,000,000 sterling, out of which £55,000,000 passed through Liverpool alone. One hundred and fifty years ago there was not a dock in England. In Liverpool they now extend over five miles in length. An hundred years hence?—and what then?

His tale being told the old man bids his readers farewell. He has chronicled a few odd matters relating to his native town. He has spoken of what it was, and of what it is. If it increase in wealth and extent during the next century as it has done in that which is past, our descendants may be so much in advance of us in wisdom and knowledge as to look slightingly upon us. But if our sons' sons will only emulate our good and graceful actions, and avoid that which in us is wicked and ignoble, they will have better reason to be proud of their ancestors than we have of ours, or even of ourselves.

# FOOTNOTES.

[167] This bridge has lately been a subject of remark, it having been laid bare in making some excavations for houses in Oxford-street. But this bridge is not the one alluded to previously which was constructed of wood, and was merely a foot-bridge, whence two paths diverged to Edge-lane and Smithdown lane.

[197] By the way, checkers on ale-house doors originated, I have been told, in a curious circumstance. They are the arms of the De Warrennes, who, at one time, had a right to grant a license to all tipsters for a certain fee. The De Warrennes arms on all house-doors indicated that the house was duly licensed. This grant was given to the De Warrennes by King John who is said to have bestowed it in recompense for breaking the head of one of the family during a game of "check" in which the King was conquered. He, in vexation, struck De Warrenne with the board. Touching these said "checkers," I once heard a good story told of a Scotch lady resident in this town. Checkers in Scotland are called "dam-boards." The lady wanting to purchase some table-cloth with a "check pattern," went into a draper's shop and asked to be shown a few. The assistant brought out several sorts, but none of them were large enough in the pattern; the lady, at length, told the young man that she wanted some of a "dam-board pattern." Not understanding the lady, but supposing she meant a d---n broad pattern, he meekly replied that they had none so broad as that!